Collins
Children's
Dictionary

Collins Children's Dictionary

David Smith and Derek Newton

Illustrated by Clifford Bayly

Picture research by Jean Bayly

Edited by
Anne Scott and Edwin Ketley

Collins Glasgow and London

First published in this edition 1978
Published by William Collins Sons and Company Limited,
Glasgow and London

© 1978 William Collins Sons and Company Limited
Printed in Great Britain

ISBN 0 00 102113 3 (limp)
ISBN 0 00 102112 5 (cased)

Introduction

This dictionary is for young readers of seven and upwards. The right level of vocabulary for the age group has been chosen on the advice of experienced teachers and librarians. We have included words which children already know or have nearly mastered, and those they can be expected to meet in reading, learning and conversation.

The definitions are clear and accurate, written in language which children can understand. Where more than one definition is given, the different meanings are clearly numbered. Some difficult definitions have a sentence using the word to give the child a better understanding of its use and meaning.

Layout and overall presentation have been planned by expert typographers, with size and style of type specially chosen to help children find correct spellings and meanings easily.

The beautifully drawn illustrations are meticulously accurate, and provide instant recognition for many of the words. The pictures are also fascinating to look at, and children will open the book again and again just to enjoy them.

Watch your children using this book, and judge how well we have succeeded in providing a proper dictionary with the appeal of a picture story book.

The Editors

Aa

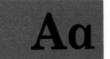

accident

accordion

abbey   1. a church.
2. a place where monks or nuns live.

aborigines   1. the first people to live in a country.
2. the original people of Australia.

about   1. nearly.
It is *about* 5 o'clock.
2. to do with.
A dictionary is a book *about* words.

abroad   across the sea; away in another country.

absent   not here; away.

accident   something happening by chance.

accordion   a musical instrument with bellows and keys.
The keys are pressed with the right hand while the left presses buttons and also moves the bellows backwards and forwards.

ache   a lasting pain like tooth*ache*.

acorn   the nut or fruit of an oak tree.

acrobat   one who does balancing tricks and exercises, usually in a circus.

across   1. from one side to the other.
He walked *across* the road.
2. on the other side of.
The school is *across* the park.

act   1. to do something.
He had to *act* quickly to catch the thief.
2. to pretend; to play a part.
John likes to *act* in the school play.
3. a law passed by a parliament.
4. a part of a stage play.
5. a deed; something done.

active   full of life; busy.

actor   a man who takes part in a play or film.

actress   a woman who takes part in a play or film.

add   to put together to make more.
Four *add* two makes six.

adder   a poisonous snake.

address 1. the place where someone lives.
2. to speak to.

admire to think very highly of.
People *admire* brave men and women.

adore to love very much.

adrift floating helplessly to and fro.

advance to move forward.

adventure an exciting or dangerous happening.

advice what we say to people to try to help them.
My *advice* is that you should not buy that puppy.

advise to give people advice; to tell other people what we think they should do.
I *advise* you not to buy that puppy.

adrift

aerial metal rod or wire. It is used to help send or pick up radio or television signals.

aeroplane flying machine with wings, heavier than air.

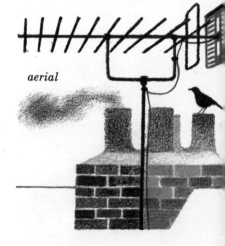

aerial

affection great liking or love.

afford to have enough money to buy something.
My father can *afford* a new car.

afraid frightened; full of fear.

after 1. at a later time.
I will go to bed *after* supper.
2. behind.
The dog ran *after* the cat.

afternoon the time between midday and evening.

again once more.
John had to do his work *again*, because it was untidy.

aeroplane

against 1. touching upon; next to.
The ladder was *against* the wall.
2. opposite to.
Our team played *against* another school.

age 1. the number of years someone has lived.
2. a special time in history, like the Iron Age.

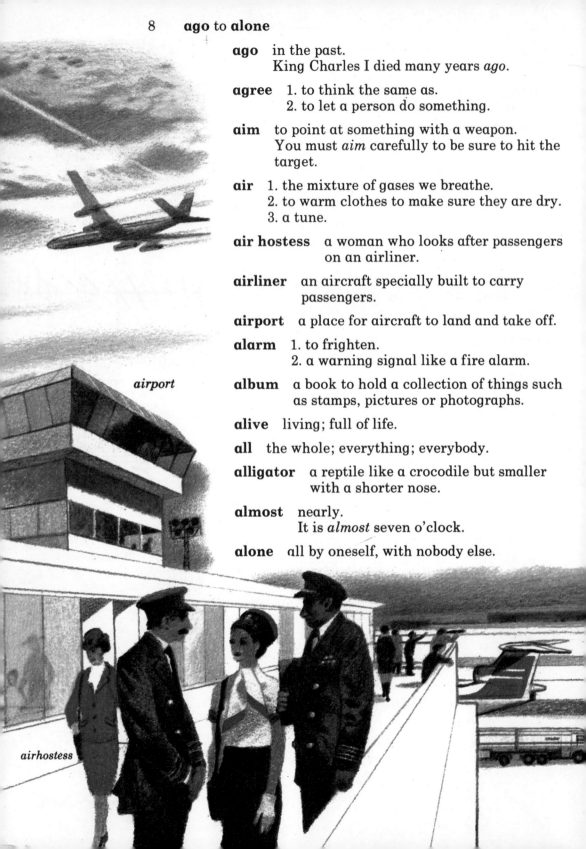

ago   in the past.
King Charles I died many years *ago*.

agree   1. to think the same as.
2. to let a person do something.

aim   to point at something with a weapon.
You must *aim* carefully to be sure to hit the target.

air   1. the mixture of gases we breathe.
2. to warm clothes to make sure they are dry.
3. a tune.

air hostess   a woman who looks after passengers on an airliner.

airliner   an aircraft specially built to carry passengers.

airport   a place for aircraft to land and take off.

alarm   1. to frighten.
2. a warning signal like a fire alarm.

airport

album   a book to hold a collection of things such as stamps, pictures or photographs.

alive   living; full of life.

all   the whole; everything; everybody.

alligator   a reptile like a crocodile but smaller with a shorter nose.

almost   nearly.
It is *almost* seven o'clock.

alone   all by oneself, with nobody else.

airhostess

along   from one end to the other.
John walked *along* the street.

aloud   able to be heard.
The teacher read *aloud* to her class.

alphabet   all the letters in a language put in a special order.
The *alphabet* has twenty-six letters.

already   by this time.
It is six o'clock *already*.

also   as well as; too.
I am eight and my friend Peter is eight *also*.

altar   1. the holy table in a church.
2. a raised place where offerings are made to a god.

alter   to make a change in something.

altogether   counting everybody and everything.
Altogether ten fish were caught.

always   at all times, for ever.

ambulance   a car or van used for taking sick or injured people to hospital.

amen   the last word of a hymn or prayer. It means 'so be it'.

among/amongst   in the middle of; with a number of other things.
There was a bad apple *among* the fruit.

amount   1. a sum of money.
2. the total of several things.

airliner

amuse to make someone feel cheerful and happy. Funny stories *amuse* people.

anchor a heavy metal hook on a long chain dropped in the sea to stop a ship moving.

ancient very old; of times long ago.

angel a messenger from God.

angry in a bad temper; very cross.

animal anything living and able to move. A bird is an *animal*, and so are fish, mammals, insects and reptiles.

anchor

ankle the joint between the foot and the knee. It allows the foot to move.

annoy to tease and make someone cross.

annual
1. once a year.
   My birthday is an *annual* event.
2. a book which comes out once a year.
3. a plant which only lives for one year.

anorak a waterproof jacket with a hood. It usually fastens with a zip.

another
1. not the same; different.
2. one more.

anvil

answer what we say or write when we are asked a question.

ant a busy small insect that lives with many other ants.

antelope an animal like a deer with long horns.

anvil an iron block on which a blacksmith hammers pieces of metal into shape.

ape

any/anything one or some out of a number of things.

ape a large monkey without a tail.

appearance
1. the way something looks. New clothes can change a person's *appearance*.
2. coming into sight. On the *appearance* of the police, the thieves ran away.

appetite the feeling of wanting food.

apple   a round fruit which grows on a tree. It has a red, green or yellow skin.

apricot   a round, yellow fruit which looks like a small peach.

April   the fourth month of the year; it has thirty days.

apron   a piece of clothing worn over the front of the body to protect the clothes.

aquarium   a place where fish, water plants and water animals are kept. It is usually a tank with glass sides, filled with water.

arch   the curved top of a door, bridge or window.

archer   someone who uses a bow and arrows.

architect   a person who plans new buildings.

area   the size of a flat space or surface.
The *area* of the floor was 9 square metres.

argue   to talk about something with a person who thinks differently, giving your reasons.

arithmetic   working with numbers, as in adding, subtracting, multiplying and dividing.

ark   1. the large boat which Noah built.
2. in the Bible, a box or chest.

arm   1. the part of the body between the shoulder and hand.
2. to give someone a weapon.

armour   a covering, usually of metal, worn to protect the body when fighting.

army   a large number, usually of soldiers.

arrange   1. to put in a special order.
2. to plan.
He will *arrange* the holiday.

arrive   to reach the place where one is going.
The train will *arrive* at noon.

arrow   a stick with a sharp tip, shot from a bow.

art   1. a special skill.
2. drawing, painting or sculpture.

aquarium

armour

ass

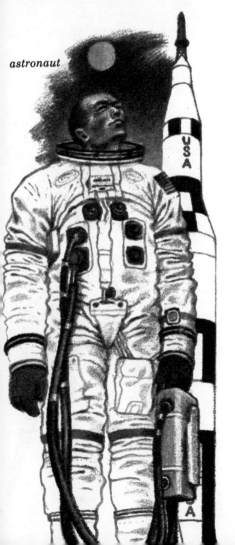

astronaut

article 1. a thing on its own.
2. a piece of writing for a newspaper or a magazine.

artist a person who paints, draws or carves.

ascend to go up; to climb.

ash 1. what is left after something has been burned.
2. a kind of tree.

ask to try to find out something from a person.

asleep not awake.
The baby was *asleep* in the pram.

ass 1. a small, long-eared animal rather like a horse.
2. a stupid person (slang).

astonish to surprise someone.

astronaut a person who travels through space in a spaceship.

atlas a book of maps.

atmosphere the air around the earth.

attack to begin to fight; set upon.
Cats *attack* mice.

attic a room just under the roof of a building.

attractive charming; being able to make people want to be near you.

audience one or more than one person watching or listening to a play, a film or a talk.

August the eighth month of the year. It has thirty-one days.

aunt a sister of a father or mother.

autumn the season between summer and winter when most fruits ripen.

avalanche a large mass of snow and ice sliding down a mountain.

avenue a street with trees lining both sides.

awake not asleep.

awe great fear and wonder.
To be in *awe* is to admire or fear someone greatly.

awful 1. dreadful; very bad.
2. causing fear or awe.

awkward 1. clumsy, not able to move quickly.
2. difficult to handle.

axe a tool with a long handle with a sharp blade at the end, for chopping wood.

axle the bar or rod on which a wheel or wheels turn.

axle

Bb

baboon a large monkey with a short tail.

baby a very young child.

back 1. not the front; upper or rear part.
Tony had a ride on the *back* of a donkey.
2. in return.
Sally paid *back* the money she owed.

bacon meat from a pig, salted and smoked.

bad 1. not good.
2. spoiled.

badge a sign; usually worn to show that a person belongs to a school, class or club.
The soldier wears a *badge* on his cap.

badger a grey, black and white striped animal about the size of a small dog. It digs holes in the ground for its home.
A *badger* lives in a sett.

bag a container made of paper, cloth, or plastic for carrying or holding things.

bait food put on a hook or in a trap to catch fish or animals.

bake to cook food in an oven.

baker a person who makes and sells bread, pies and cakes.

balance 1. to keep steady.
2. a machine for weighing.

balance

ballet

barge

bald   having no hair.

ball   anything round, like an orange.

ballet   a special kind of dancing; the dancers and music tell a story.

balloon   a very thin rubber bag which can be blown up so that it floats above the ground.

ball-point   a pen with a tiny ball at the end for writing with.

bamboo   a very tall grass with stiff hollow stems. *Bamboo* is used for garden canes and for furniture.

banana   a long, thin fruit with a yellow skin.

band   1. a number of people who play music together.
2. a thin strip of something, like an elastic *band*.

bandage   1. a strip of cloth used to cover and tie up a wound.
2. to wrap up an injury.

bandit   a robber who steals from travellers.

banister   the rail to hold at the side of the stairs.

banjo   a musical instrument, played by plucking the strings.

bank   1. a building where people put their money so that it will be safe.
2. the ground at the river's edge.
3. a mound or heap of earth covered with grass.

bar   1. a long piece of metal.
2. a counter where food and drink are sold.

barber   a man who cuts hair.

bare   not covered; with nothing on.
The child's *bare* feet were cold.

barge   a flat-bottomed boat used to carry goods, usually on canals and rivers.

bark   1. the cry of a dog.
2. the outside covering of trees.

barn   a large building where a farmer stores hay, grain and other crops.

barrel   1. a round wooden container.
2. the tube-like part of a gun.

barrow   a small cart with one wheel that is pushed by hand.

base   the bottom of something; the part on which something stands or is built.

barn

basket   a kind of bag made from thin pieces of wood or straw, used for carrying things.

bat   1. a piece of wood used to hit the ball in some games.
2. an animal like a mouse with wings, which flies at night.

bath   a large container in which to wash the body.

bathe   to wash, play or swim in water.

bathroom   the room where the bath or shower is.

battery   a container for storing electricity.
Jack needs a *battery* for his electric clock and Susan needs a *battery* for her radio.

battle   a fight between armies, ships or aeroplanes during a war.

cricket bat

baseball bat

bay   a stretch of sea water curving into the land.

beach   the sand or pebbles at the edge of the sea or a lake.

beacon   a light, like a lighthouse or bonfire, used as a signal.

bead   a small round piece of wood or glass or stone. It can be threaded with others to make a necklace.

beak   the hard, pointed or curved part of a bird's mouth.

beaker   a tall cup sometimes without a handle.

bean   a vegetable with large seeds that grow in pods.

bear

beaver

beehive

bee

bear   a large, heavy animal with thick fur.
A polar *bear* is white.

beard   hair growing on a man's face.

beast   any animal.

beautiful   very pretty; lovely; very pleasing to
see or hear.

beaver   a small, furry animal that lives near
water. It has a wide, flat tail and webbed
hind feet.

because   for the reason that; as.
Sally cannot go to school *because* she
is ill.

bed   1. something to lie and sleep on.
2. a place where plants are grown.
3. the bottom of the sea or a river.

bedroom   the room where the bed is.

bee   a flying insect that makes honey and wax.
It can also sting.

beech   a large tree with dark, shiny leaves.

beef   meat from a cow or bull.

beehive   a house for bees.

beer   a strong drink made from malt, barley and
hops.

beetle   an insect that has four wings and a hard
skin.

beetroot   a dark-red, root vegetable.

before   earlier than; in front of.
Look *before* you cross the road.

beg   to ask for food, clothes or money.
The poor old lady had to *beg* for food.

beggar   someone who begs.

begin   to start.
Schools usually *begin* at nine.

behave   1. to act or to do.
Why do you *behave* like that?
2. to be good in front of others.

behind   at the back of.
Tom hid *behind* the fence.

believe   1. to think that something is true.
2. to think someone tells the truth.

bell   a piece of metal shaped like a cup. It makes a ringing sound when struck.

bellow   to roar loudly.

belong   1. to be your own.
Does this book *belong* to you?
2. to be part of.

below   underneath, lower than.

belt   a long strip of cloth, leather or plastic usually for supporting or linking things, or to wear round the waist.

bench   a long seat, usually made of wood.
Carol sat on a *bench* in the park.

bend   to make something curved or crooked.
The tree began to *bend* in the wind.

beret (say *berray*)   a soft, round, flat hat.

berry   a small, juicy fruit with seeds.

berth   a bed or a bunk in a train or a ship.

beside   at the side of, close to.

best   none better.
Mary's picture is the *best* in the class.

between   in the middle of two things.
Tim sat *between* his mother and father.

beware   to be careful about something that might be dangerous.
Beware of the ice on that pond.

Bible   a holy book about the history of the Jews and the life of Jesus Christ.

bicycle   a vehicle to ride, with two wheels and pedals to make them turn.

big   large.

billy-goat   a male goat.

bind   to tie or fasten together.

bells

berth

bicycle

bison

blacksmith

blast-off

bingo   a game of lucky numbers usually played by lots of people at once, in a hall or club.

bird   an animal that has wings and feathers.

birthday   the day of the year when a person is born.

biscuit   a thin, small cake baked hard.

bison   a kind of wild buffalo or ox.

bit   a small piece.

bite   to cut with the teeth.
The dog tried to *bite* the postman.

black   very dark, without any light.

blackberry   a small juicy fruit which often grows in hedgerows; the bramble.

blackbird   a songbird with black feathers and a yellow beak.

blackboard   a smooth board, usually black, for writing or drawing on with chalk.

blackcurrant   a small, black fruit that grows on a garden bush.

blacksmith   a man who works with iron or a man who mends and makes iron things.
A *blacksmith* makes horseshoes.

blade   1. the part of a knife for cutting things.
2. one leaf of grass.

blame   to find fault with.
Sam was to *blame* for breaking the window.

blancmange   a kind of jelly made with milk.

blanket   a thick, warm cloth usually made of wool.
A *blanket* is used as a bed-cover.

blast-off   the moment a space-ship or rocket leaves the ground.

blaze   1. a bright fire.
2. to burn brightly.

bleat   the cry of a sheep or goat.

birds

herring gull

night heron

Canada goose

swallow

golden eagle

humming bird

black vulture

puffin

eagle owl

emperor penguin

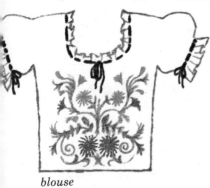

blouse

bluebell

bluebottle

bollard

bleed to lose blood.
If you cut your hand it will *bleed*.

blind 1. not able to see.
2. a screen to keep out light.

blindfold 1. a cover for the eyes to stop a person seeing.
2. to cover the eyes.

blizzard a snowstorm with strong wind.

block 1. a big piece of wood, stone or metal.
2. to be in the way of something.

blond/blonde a person with fair hair.

blood the red liquid in the body needed to live.

blot a spot or mark usually made by ink.

blouse clothing worn by women and girls on the top part of the body.

blow 1. to send air out of the mouth.
Watch Heather *blow* hard to put out the candle.
2. a hard knock.

blue a colour.

bluebell a wild plant with blue flowers shaped like bells.

bluebottle a large fly with a blue body.

blunt not sharp.
You can't cut with those *blunt* scissors.

board 1. a long, flat piece of wood.
2. to get on a plane, boat or train.

boat a small ship.

body all the parts together of a person or animal.

boil 1. to heat water so that it bubbles and gives off steam.
2. a very painful swelling on the body.

bollard a strong post on a pavement or pedestrian crossing; also found on piers and docks.

bones the hard, white parts inside the body.

bonfire   a fire lit outside.
They lit a *bonfire* in the garden.

book   pages of paper fastened together in a cover. Words and pictures are usually printed on the pages.

boomerang   a curved weapon of Australia made out of wood. It turns in the air and comes back to the person who throws it.

boot   a kind of shoe that covers part of the leg as well as the foot, often made of leather or rubber.

bore   1. to make a hole in wood, metal or other materials, by using a drill.
2. to talk in an uninteresting way.

born   at the beginning of life.
Peter was *born* in Leeds ten years ago.

borrow   to take something that will have to be given back.
May I *borrow* your ball please?

boss   a chief, someone in charge.

both   the two together.
Both your hands are dirty!

bottle   a container for liquids.
A *bottle* holds milk, lemonade or other liquids.

bottom   the lowest part.
The diver worked on the *bottom* of the sea.

bough (as in **now**)   a branch of a tree.

bounce   to spring up and down.
See how many times the ball can *bounce*.

bouquet (say *bookay*)   a bunch of flowers.

bow (as in **so**)   1. a kind of knot used to tie ribbon or shoe laces.
2. a weapon used for shooting arrows.

bow (as in **now**)   to bend forward and lower the head.

bowl   a deep dish, usually round.

bonfire

bow

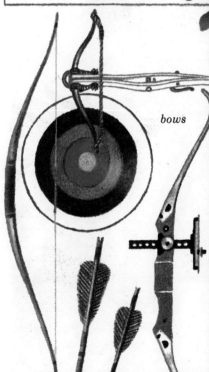

bouquet

bows

boxer

bracelet

bricklayer

box a container with straight sides.

boxer a man who fights another man with his fists, usually in a competition.

boy a male child.

bracelet a band or chain worn round the arm or wrist.

brake the part of a vehicle or any machine that slows it down or stops it.
The *brake* squealed when it was put on.

bramble a blackberry bush.

branch the part of a tree that grows from the main stem.

brass a yellow-coloured metal.

brave 1. not being afraid.
2. a North American Indian warrior.

bray the cry of a donkey.

bread a food made from flour and baked in an oven.

break 1. to smash.
If you drop the eggs they will *break*.
2. a rest.
I shall have a *break* when I finish my work.

breakfast the first meal of the day.

breath air that is drawn into and let out of the body by the lungs.
Take a deep *breath* before you dive into the water.

breathe to take air into the body and let it out again.

breeze a light wind.

brewery a place where beer is made.

brick a block of baked clay used in building.

bricklayer a man who builds with bricks.

bride a woman on her wedding day.

bridegroom a man on his wedding day.

bridesmaid   a woman usually not married who helps the bride on her wedding day.

bridge   something built over a river, road or railway to make it easy to cross to the other side.

brief   short; not long.

bright   1. shining, sending out light. Jane covered her eyes because the sun was so *bright*.
2. clever.

brim   1. the edge of a cup, bowl or glass.
2. the part of a hat that sticks out all round.

bring   to fetch or carry something.

brittle   easily broken.

broad   wide.
The bridge spanned the *broad* river.

broadcast   to send out programmes such as music, news or plays by radio or television.

brooch   an ornament to pin on clothes.

brook   a small stream.

broom   a hard brush with a long handle, used for sweeping floors.

brother   a boy is *brother* to the other children of his mother and father.

brown   a dark colour, like that of chocolate or coffee.

brush   1. hair or bristles fixed to a handle, used for cleaning, painting, doing the hair or cleaning the teeth.
2. to rub.

bubble   1. a thin ball of liquid with air or gas inside.
2. to froth.

bucket   a container with a handle for holding or carrying water.

buckle   a fastening on a belt or shoe.

bud   a young leaf or flower before it opens.

bridge

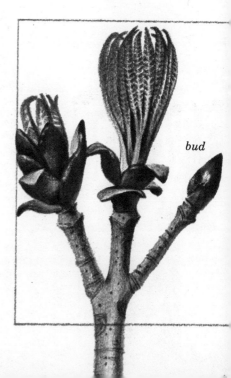

bud

bulldozer

budgerigar   a brightly coloured bird, like a very small parrot, often kept as a pet.

buffalo   a wild ox.

bugle   a musical instrument like a small trumpet. It is used in the army to call soldiers.

build   to make something; to put something together.
People *build* houses and ships.

building   something that is built, such as a house, shop or church.

bulb   1. the round root, often shaped like an onion, from which flowers grow.
A tulip grows from a *bulb*.
2. the glass of an electric light.

bull   the male of cattle and some other animals. A male elephant is also called a *bull*.

bulldog   a kind of dog, strong and brave.

bulldozer   a very powerful tractor with a large steel blade at the front to push loads of earth.

bullet   a small piece of metal shot from a gun to wound or kill.

buildings

The Acropolis Athens

St Basil's Moscow

St Paul's London

Tower of London

bully   a person who hurts or frightens weaker people.

bulrush   a tall thin plant that grows in or near water.

bump   1. to knock against something or someone.
2. a swelling often caused by a blow.
He fell and now has a *bump* on his head.

bun   a small, soft cake, usually round.

bunch   a group of things growing or fastened together.

bundle   several things tied or wrapped together.

bungalow   a house with all its rooms on the ground floor.

bunk   a bed, for one person, fixed to the wall in a ship's cabin.

buoy   a marker floating in the sea and fastened to the sea bed. It marks dangerous rocks, wrecks, or a safe channel for ships.

burglar   a person who breaks into buildings and steals things.

buoy

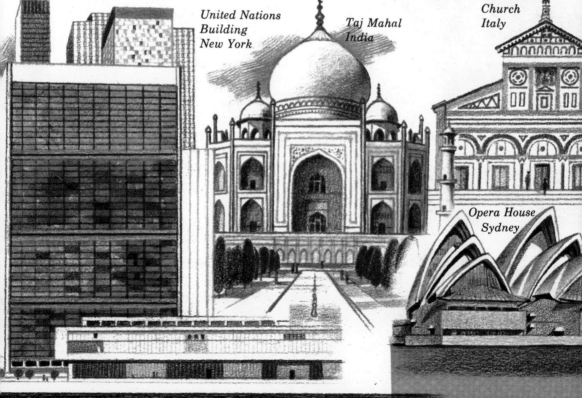

United Nations Building New York

Taj Mahal India

Florentine Church Italy

Opera House Sydney

Ulysses, Australia

Fiery Acrea, Africa

Large Blue, Asia

Peacock, Europe

butterflies

burn 1. to be on fire.
2. an injury caused by heat or fire.

burrow a hole in the ground dug by wild animals and used as their home.

burst 1. to break open suddenly.
If you blow too hard a balloon will *burst*.
2. a sudden movement forward.

bury to put something in the ground and cover it up.

bus a large coach for carrying people from place to place.

bush 1. a small tree, usually with many branches, growing near the ground.
2. uncultivated land in Australia and Africa.

bus stop a place in the street or road where people can get on or off a bus.

busy having plenty to do.
The children are *busy* writing and drawing.

butcher a man who cuts up meat and sells it.

butter a soft, yellow food made from cream.

buttercup a small, yellow, wild flower.

butterfly an insect with four large wings.

button 1. a fastening for clothes.
2. any small knob.

buy to get something by giving money for it; to purchase.

Cc

cactus

cab 1. the place in a bus, truck or train where the driver sits.
2. a taxi.

cabbage a vegetable with thick, green leaves. It can be eaten raw or cooked.

cabin 1. a room for passengers on a ship or an aeroplane.
2. a small hut usually made of wood.

cactus a prickly plant which grows wild in hot desert countries.

café a place where meals or snacks are sold; a tea or coffee house.

cage a room or box fitted with wires or bars. Birds or other animals are sometimes kept in a *cage*.

cake a sweet kind of food made from flour and baked in an oven.

calendar a list of all the days and dates in each month of the year.

calf 1. a young bull or cow.
2. the back of the leg below the knee.

call 1. to shout or cry out.
2. to make a telephone *call*.
3. to go to someone's house.
4. to give a name to someone.
We *call* him Peter.

calm quiet and still.

camel a large animal with either one or two humps on its back.
The *camel* is used to carry people and goods in hot, dry lands.

camera a machine used to take photographs.

camp 1. to live in a tent out of doors.
2. a place where tents are set up.
The scouts made their *camp* near a farm.

can 1. a metal container, usually round.
A *can* of soup fell and rolled off the table.
2. to be allowed to.
Mother says that John *can* go to the party.
3. to be able to.
Can you swim?

canal a very large, man-made ditch dug across land and filled with water to join places.
Ships, boats and barges sail along a *canal*.

canary a small, yellow, singing bird often kept as a pet.

candle a stick of wax with a wick in the middle, which is burned to give light.

cannon a large gun, sometimes on wheels.

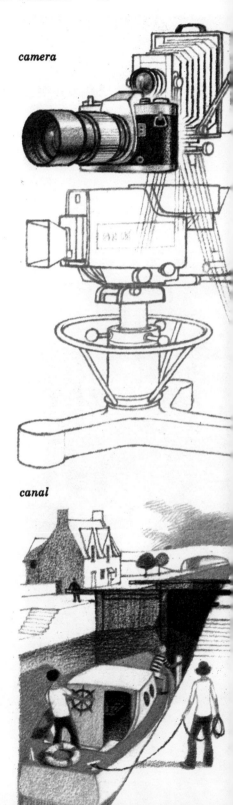

camera

canal

canoes

carnival

canoe   a small, light boat moved with paddles.

cap   1. a small, soft hat with a peak at the front.
2. a lid.

capital   1. the chief city of a country.
London is the *capital* of England.
2. a large letter of the alphabet.
A is a *capital* letter; *a* is a small letter.

capsize   to overturn.
Sit down or you may *capsize* the boat.

capsule   1. a spacecraft; the cabin of a spacecraft.
2. a small container for medicine.

captain   1. the man in charge of a ship.
2. the leader of a team.
Jill is *captain* of the netball team.
3. an officer in an army.

capture   to take a prisoner, to catch.
The boys tried to *capture* the lost dog.

car   a motor vehicle used by people to drive from
place to place.

caravan   a small house on wheels often pulled by
a car.
Peter and his family stayed in a *caravan*
at the seaside.

card   a flat piece of stiff paper.

cardboard   stiff board made of paper.

cardigan   a short knitted jacket.

care   1. caution; paying attention to.
Take *care* when you cross the road.
2. to look after.
If you are ill your mother will *care* for you.

careful   taking care.

caretaker   someone who looks after a building
such as a school.

cargo   goods carried by a ship or an aircraft.

carnation   a garden flower with a pleasing smell.

carnival   a gay time; a happy, jolly party or
parade often in fancy dress.

carol   a song of joy.
   We sang a *carol* at Christmas.

carpenter   a person who makes things out of wood.

carpet   a thick woven covering for the floor.

carriage   a room on wheels for carrying people from place to place.
   We sat in a *carriage* on the train.

carrot   a root vegetable, orange in colour.

carry   to take from one place to another.

cart   a wagon, usually with two wheels, used for carrying goods.

carton   a box usually made of card or cardboard.
   The rulers were packed in a *carton*.

cartoon   1. a kind of comic drawing.
   2. a short, funny film made with drawings.

case   a box to keep or carry things in.
   Ann packed her *case* ready for the holiday.

cash   money in coins and banknotes.

cask   a barrel or tub to hold liquids.

castle   an old building with thick stone walls and towers, built to keep out the enemy.

cat   a small, furry animal often kept as a pet in houses.

catapult   a Y-shaped stick with elastic tied to it, used for firing stones.

catch   1. to take hold of something which is moving.
   Catch the ball with both hands.
   2. a kind of lock.
   Put the *catch* on the gate when you leave.

caterpillar   a grub which turns into a butterfly or moth.

cathedral   a very large church; the most important church in a district.

catkin   the fluffy flower of the willow, hazel and some other trees.

carriages

castle

maize

cereal

rice

barley

wheat

oats

cattle   farm animals such as bulls, cows and calves.

cauliflower   a vegetable with a large, white part in the middle. The white part is usually cooked and eaten.

cavalry   soldiers who ride horses.

cave   a large hole in the rock, or in the side of a hill, or underground.

cedar   an evergreen tree which grows cones.

ceiling   the inside roof of a room.
Look up at the *ceiling*, look down at the floor.

celery   a vegetable with long, white stems and pale green leaves. It can be eaten.

cellar   a room under the ground.

cement   a grey-white powder which becomes hard when mixed with sand and water.
Cement is used to stick bricks together and in making concrete.

centimetre   a short measure of length. One hundred centimetres equal one metre.

centipede   a crawling insect that has many legs.

centre   the middle point.

century   1. one hundred years.
2. one hundred runs in cricket.

cereal   1. any grain used as food.
2. breakfast food.

certain   sure.
It is *certain* that 7 add 2 do not equal 10.

certificate   a handwritten or printed paper saying something is true.
Sally has a *certificate* to prove she can swim 50 metres.

chain   rings of metal joined together.

chair   a single seat with a back.

chalk   a soft, white stone that is used for writing on a blackboard.

champion   the winner; the best.
Sally won the cup as swimming *champion* of the school.

chance   1. luck; something not planned.
There is a *chance* that John will win a prize.
2. opportunity.

change   1. to make different; to alter.
2. money given back when too much is offered to pay for something.

channel   a narrow stretch of water between two pieces of land.

chapel   1. a small church.
2. part of a large church.

charm   1. to be pleasing to someone.
2. a spell.

chart   1. a kind of map used on ships.
2. a sheet of facts.

chase   to run after.

chat   to talk in a friendly way.

chauffeur   a person who is paid to drive a car.

cheap   costing only a little money.

check   1. to make sure something is right.
Will you *check* that the windows are shut?
2. a pattern with squares on it.
3. to slow down or stop.
The rider had to *check* his horse's speed to jump the high fence.

cheek   1. the soft part of the face between the nose and the ear.
2. bad manners.

cheerful   happy; glad.

cheese   a food made from milk.

cheetah   a large wild cat which can run very quickly.

chemist   a person who makes up medicines.
One can buy medicines, toothpaste and soap from the *chemist*.

chauffeur

cheetah

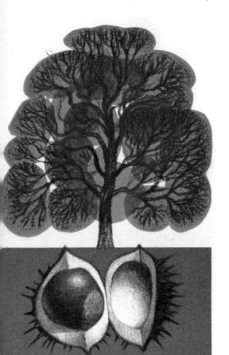

horse chestnut

chimpanzee

cherry   a small, round fruit with a hard seed in the middle.

chess   a game for two people played with special pieces on a board marked out in squares.

chest   1. a large, strong box with a lid.
2. the front part of the body between the waist and the neck.

chestnut   a large tree and its brown shiny nut.

chew   to crush and grind with the teeth.

chicken   1. a young hen or cock.
2. the meat of a young hen or cock.

chief   1. a leader.
The Indian *chief* spoke to the cowboys
2. most important.

child   a young boy or girl.

children   young boys and girls.

chimney   a kind of tube that takes away smoke from a fire.

chimpanzee   an ape, smaller than a gorilla.

china   cups, saucers and plates made from a special kind of white clay.

chips   1. thin slices of potato fried in oil or fat.
2. pieces cut or broken off.

chirp   a short, high sound often made by birds.

chisel   1. a sharp tool used for cutting wood or stone.
2. to cut or shape with a chisel.

chocolate   a brown sweet or a hot drink made from cocoa, milk and sugar.

choir   1. a group of singers.
2. part of the church occupied by the choir.

choke   1. to find it hard to breathe.
2. to block up.

choose   to pick out.

chop   1. to cut with an axe.
2. a piece of meat.

Christian   a person who follows the teachings of Jesus Christ.

Christmas   the time of year when the birth of Jesus Christ is celebrated.

church   a building where people pray to God.

churchyard   the ground around a church.

cigarette   tobacco rolled in thin paper for smoking.

cinema   a place where films are shown.

circle   a ring; a perfect round shape.

circus   a travelling show held in a tent or building, with animals, clowns and acrobats.

city   a very large town.

clap   1. to slap the hands together to show pleasure.
2. a noise.
A *clap* of thunder made us all jump.

class   1. a group of children who are taught together.
2. a group of people or things which are alike.

classroom   a room in a school where children learn.

claw   a sharp, hooked nail on the foot of a bird or animal.

clay   soft, sticky earth that is used to make bricks and pottery.

clean   washed; not dirty.

clear   1. open; with nothing in the way.
The snow has been moved so the roads are now *clear*.
2. easy to see through, such as a window.
3. to pass without touching.
She jumped high to *clear* the bar.

clerk   a person who works in an office.

clever   quick to learn.

cliff   a very steep, almost straight hillside, often near the sea.

circus

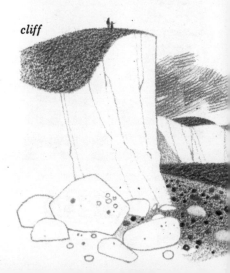

cliff

cloak

climate   the kind of weather a place has.

climb   to go up, sometimes using hands and feet to hold on.

clinic   a place where people are helped by doctors and nurses.

clip   1. to fasten together.
2. to cut short.
The farmers *clip* wool from the sheep.

cloak   a loose coat with no sleeves.

cloakroom   a place to leave outdoor clothes.

clock   a machine for telling the time.

close (as in **toes**)   1. to shut.
Please *close* the door, it's cold.
2. to end.
The concert will *close* with the National Anthem.

close (as in **dose**)   1. very near.
Stay *close* together, the path is narrow.
2. stuffy; without air.
If the room is *close*, open a window.

clothes   things to wear.

cloud   1. very many tiny drops of water floating close together in the sky.
2. a large amount of smoke, steam or dust.

clover   a small, wild plant with white or pink flowers and small leaves growing in threes.

clown   a funny man usually in a circus.

club   1. a heavy stick.
2. a group of people who meet to do things together.

clumsy   awkward.
Alan was very *clumsy* because he knocked over the vase of flowers.

coach   1. a carriage for people travelling by road or rail.
2. an instructor especially in games.
3. to train usually in games.

clocks

coal a kind of hard, black rock dug out of the ground.
Coal is burned to give off heat.

coarse rough; thick, not fine.

coast the seashore; where the sea and land meet.

coat an outer covering.
Ann wore her *coat* because it was cold.
The house needs a *coat* of paint.
A sheep's *coat* is called a fleece.

cobbler a person who mends shoes and boots.

cobra a poisonous snake.

cobweb a net made by a spider to trap insects.

cock a male bird.

cockle a shell fish.

cockpit the place where a pilot sits in an aircraft; the driver's seat in a racing car.

cocoa brown powder made from the fruit (beans) of the cacao tree.

coconut a very large, round nut, which grows on the coco palm tree.

cod a large sea fish eaten as food.

coffee a hot drink made from the roasted seeds of the coffee bush.

coin a piece of money, made of metal.

cold 1. not hot.
Ice is *cold*.
2. an illness of the nose and throat.

collar a part of clothing worn round the neck.

collect to bring together.
John and Joyce *collect* stamps.

college a place for learning, usually after leaving school.

collide to bang, to bump together by mistake.

colonel a senior officer in the army.

colour a dye; paint.
John's favourite *colour* is red.

coal

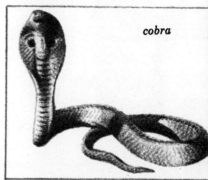

cobra

cockpit

colt   a young male horse.

comb   a short piece of plastic or metal with teeth, used to keep the hair tidy.

combine-harvester   a farm machine that cuts and threshes grain.

come   to move near.

comedian   someone who makes people laugh.

comic   1. a picture paper for children.
2. a funny person.

comical   very funny.

common   1. found in many places.
2. usual.
3. a public stretch of ground.
4. rude.

companion   a friend.

compare   to see if things are alike or different.

compass   an instrument which shows north, south, east and west.

compasses   an instrument for drawing circles.

complete   having all the parts; with nothing missing.

comrade   a friend; a companion.

concert   a musical show played in front of people.

concrete   a hard, dried mixture of cement, stones, sand and water.

conductor   1. the person in charge of passengers on a bus or train.
2. the person who stands in front of an orchestra and keeps or beats time.

cone   1. a solid shape rounded at the bottom and pointed at the top.
2. fruit (seeds) of trees like the pine or cedar.
3. a container for ice-cream.

confuse   to mistake one thing for another; mix up.

conjurer   a person who does clever or magic tricks.

combine-harvester

compass

conker   a round, shiny, hard, brown nut in a prickly covering.
A *conker* is the nut of the horse-chestnut tree.

connect   to join together.

constable   a policeman.

construct   to build, to make.

container   a box, tin, jar or pot used to hold or contain something.

convent   a house where nuns live and work.

cook   1. a person who gets meals ready.
2. to heat food and get it ready for eating.

cooker   a gas or electric stove for cooking food.

cool   not warm but not very cold.

copper   a metal, reddish in colour.

copy   1. something made exactly like another.
2. to imitate; to make another the same.

cork   1. the light, thick bark of a kind of oak tree.
2. a stopper for a container.

corn   a grain or seed used as food.

corner   1. the place where two lines meet, or where two streets or walls meet.
2. to drive into a trap.

correct   having no mistakes, all right and true.

corridor   a passage in a building.

cosmonaut   the Russian name for a person who travels in space. .

cost   1. the price paid for something.
The *cost* of food keeps rising.
2. to be of a certain value.
A diamond ring will *cost* a lot of money.

costume   a style of dress; stage clothes worn by actors.
The kilt is part of the national *costume* of Scotland.

cot   a small bed for a baby.

cottage   a small house in the country.

North Africa

Holland

Tonga

Japan

Spain

N. America

India

Nigeria

Scotland

costume

cowboy

cranes

cotton thread or cloth made from the cotton plant.

couch a long, soft seat.

cough the noise made when someone has a cold on the chest or when choking.

count 1. to find out how many.
2. to say numbers in their correct order – 1, 2, 3, 4 and so on.
3. a nobleman.

counter 1. a kind of table in a shop over which people are served and pay.
2. a coin or disc.

country 1. land outside the towns.
2. the land where a nation of people lives. England, France, Australia and New Zealand are *countries*.

couple two; a pair.

courage the feeling of not being afraid.

cousin a close relation; the child of one's uncle or aunt.

cover 1. to put one thing over another, to hide.
2. anything that shelters.

cow an animal that gives milk.

coward a person who has no courage.

cowboy a man who lives on a ranch and looks after cattle.

crab a sea animal with a hard shell, eight legs and two big claws.

crack 1. a sharp noise.
2. a split or thin opening.
There is a *crack* in your cup.

cracker 1. a little firework.
2. a crisp kind of biscuit.

cradle a cot for a baby.

crane 1. a machine for lifting large and heavy things.
2. a large water bird with long legs.

crash 1. a loud noise of breaking.
2. an accident.
3. to hit against and be smashed.
Sally saw the car *crash* into the wall.

crawl to move on hands and knees.

crayon a stick of coloured wax or chalk, used for drawing.

cream the thick part of milk found at the top.

creature any living person or animal.
A fish is a *creature*, so is a bird and an insect.

creek 1. a place where a small stream flows into the sea.
2. part of a river or stream.

creep to move slowly and with little noise.

cress a green plant used in salads.

crew a group of people who work on a ship, aircraft or train.

cricket 1. a game played with bats, wickets and a ball between two teams of eleven players.
2. an insect that jumps and makes a high, sharp sound.

crimson a deep red colour.

crisp easily broken.

crisps very thin slices of fried potato.

crocodile a large and dangerous animal that lives in or near rivers in hot countries.

crocus a small plant that flowers in spring.

crooked not straight.

crop 1. food such as fruit, vegetables and corn grown on the land.
2. to cut.

cross 1. a shape like + or ×.
2. angry.
3. to go from one side to another.

crow a large, black bird with a harsh call.

cricket

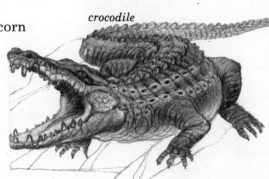

crocodile

crown

crowd   a large number of people together in one place.

crown   1. the jewelled head-dress of a king or queen.
2. the top.

cruel   very unkind to people and animals.

crumb   a very small piece of bread or cake.

crush   to squeeze together very hard.

crust   the hard, outside part, such as a crust of bread.

cry   1. to shout out.
2. to let tears fall from the eyes.
Jack began to *cry* when he fell down.

cub   a young animal such as a fox, wolf or lion.

cube   a solid shape with six equal faces.

cuckoo   a bird that lays its eggs in the nests of other birds.

cucumber   a long, green vegetable used in salads.

cup   a small bowl with a handle used for drinking.
Tea is drunk from a *cup*.

cupboard   a set of shelves with doors at the front.

cure   1. to make a sick person better again.
2. to preserve; as bacon and ham.

curious   1. wanting to find out.
2. strange.

curly   not straight.
Mary has *curly* hair.

currant   a small dried grape.

current   moving water, air, or electricity.
The children were not allowed to swim in the river because the *current* was too strong.

curtain   cloth which hangs down to cover a window.

cushion   a soft pillow for a chair.

crush

cub

custard a sauce or pudding made from milk, eggs and sugar cooked together.

customer a person who buys from a shop.

cut to make smaller pieces with a knife, scissors or a saw.

cycle 1. another word for bicycle.
2. to ride a bicycle.

cyclone a violent storm with strong winds; a hurricane.

cylinder an object shaped like a tube.

cymbals metal musical instruments shaped like large plates.

cymbals

daddy/dad a child's name for father.

daffodil a yellow, bell-shaped flower that grows from a bulb.

dagger a pointed knife shaped like a sword.

dahlia a garden flower with bright blossoms.

daily every day.

dairy a place for keeping milk and cream. Butter and cheese are made in a *dairy*.

daisy a small, wild flower with white or pink petals and a yellow centre.

dam a bank or wall, built to hold back water.

damp slightly wet.

damson a small, dark-purple plum.

dance to move about in time to music.

dandelion a wild plant with bright yellow flowers.

danger something which can do harm.

dangerous unsafe; likely to cause harm. It is *dangerous* to skate on thin ice.

dark without light.

dart 1. a small arrow for throwing.
2. to make a sudden quick movement.

Dd

dam

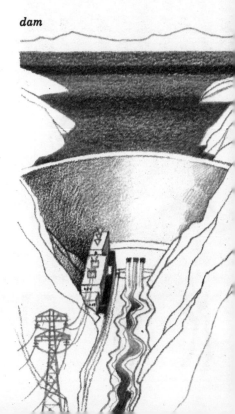

dates

dash 1. to hurry.
2. a short straight line used in writing (—).

date 1. the fruit of a palm tree.
2. the day, month and year.
The *date* of my birthday is the 6th of May.

daughter a girl child.

dawn the beginning of a day when the first light from the sun shows.

day 1. the time between sunrise and sunset.
2. twenty-four hours.

daytime the time when it is light.

dazzle to blind for a time with bright light.

dead no longer living; without life.

deaf not able to hear.

dear 1. loved very much.
The child was *dear* to her mother.
2. costing a lot of money.

deceive to make someone believe something untrue.

December the twelfth month of the year. It has thirty-one days.

decide to make up one's mind.

deck the flooring of a ship or boat.

decorate 1. to make something look pretty.
2. to give a medal.

deed something done; an act.

deep going a long way down or back.
The sea is very *deep*.

deer

deer a quick-running, grass-eating animal with four long legs. The male has long horns or antlers which look like branches.

defend to keep safe from danger.

delicious very tasty and good to eat.
Mary enjoyed a *delicious* meal.

delightful giving great joy and happiness.

deliver   1. to rescue or set free.
2. to hand over to someone else.
The postman came to *deliver* a parcel.

demon   an evil spirit; a devil.

dent   a small hollow or bend in a smooth surface.

dentist   a person who takes care of teeth.

depend   to rely on and trust someone.

deposit   1. to put down something and leave it.
2. money left in part payment for something.

depth   the distance from top to bottom.

descend   to go or climb down.
The climbers began to *descend* from the top of the mountain.

dentist

describe   to give a picture of somebody or something in words or writing.

desert   land where very little grows.

deserve   to earn something by an action.
The children who work hard *deserve* to do well.

desk   a table for writing or reading. It often has drawers.

destroy   to spoil completely.

devil   a demon; an evil spirit; a wicked person.

dew   little drops of water that cover the ground first thing in the morning.

descend

dial   1. the flat, round face with numbers on a clock, watch or telephone.
2. to make a telephone call by turning the dial.

diamond   a very hard, precious stone. When cut it sparkles brightly.

diary   a small notebook for writing daily happenings.

dictionary   a book giving the meaning of words.

die   to stop living.

diamond

dinghy

dinosaur

diesel an engine using a special kind of oil.

difference the way in which things are not the same.
The *difference* between 4 and 7 is 3.

different not the same; unlike.
A pencil is *different* from a crayon.

difficult hard; not easy.

dig to turn over soil with a spade.

dim not bright or clear.
He could not see very well in the *dim* light.

dinghy a small rowing or sailing boat.

dining-room the room where meals are eaten.

dinner the main meal of the day.

dinosaur a very large reptile which lived a very long time ago.

direct 1. straight; by the quickest or shortest way.
2. to show someone the way.

dirty needing to be washed or cleaned; not clean.

disagree to quarrel, to think differently.

disappear to go out of sight; to vanish.

disappoint to make someone unhappy by not doing what they had hoped.

disc something round and flat.

disciple a follower or pupil of a great person.
Each of the twelve followers of Jesus was called a *disciple*.

discover to find something.

discuss to talk about something.

disease an illness or sickness.

dish a shallow bowl with a rim like a plate.

dishonest not able to be trusted.

disloyal letting someone down.
The *disloyal* man gave away his friend's secret.

dismay a feeling of being upset or sad.

disobey   to do what one is told not to do; to refuse to obey.

distance   the space between two objects or places. The *distance* between the towns is 20 kilometres.

disturb   to upset or cause trouble.

ditch   a long, narrow trench dug in the ground to drain away water.

dive   to go head-first downwards, usually into water.

diver   a person who works underwater, usually in a special diving suit.

do   to carry out an action.

dock   a place where ships are loaded and unloaded.

doctor   a person who takes care of sick people.

dodge   to move quickly out of the way.

doe   a female deer.

dog   a four-legged animal related to the wolf. It is often kept as a pet.

Alsatian

Boxer

dogs

Bulldog

Afghan hound

Chow Chow

Chihuahua

Airedale terrier

Bearded collie

Dachshund

dogfish

dove

dragon

dogfish a kind of small shark.

doll a model of a real person used as a toy.

dollar a unit of money in some countries such as Australia, New Zealand and Canada.

donkey a long-eared animal like a small horse; another name for an ass.

door a barrier to be opened to enter a room or building.

doorstep the step in front of the outside door.

doorway the way into a building.

dose the amount to be taken at one time, usually of medicine.
The *dose* is one spoonful taken twice a day.

double 1. to make twice as big.
2. to fold over.

doubt to be unsure about something.

dough a thick, floury mixture.

doughnut a circular cake made of a thick, floury mixture covered with sugar and often with a hole in the middle.

dove a kind of pigeon.

down 1. at or to a lower place.
Fred came *down* from the top of the tower.
2. soft hair or feathers.

dozen a group of twelve.

drag to pull slowly and heavily.

dragon in fairy tales, a winged animal breathing fire.

dragonfly an insect with two pairs of wings.

drain 1. a pipe to run off waste water.
2. to run off waste water.

draper a person who sells things made of cloth.

draught a stream of air.

draughts a game played with round counters on a special square board.

draw to make a picture with crayon, pencil or chalk.

drawbridge a bridge that can be lifted up or let down.
There is often a *drawbridge* near the gate of a castle.

drawer a box that slides in and out of a piece of furniture.

drawing-pin a pin with a large, flat head.

dreadful terrible; making someone very afraid.

dream the pictures and thoughts in the mind during sleep.

dress 1. clothing worn by ladies or girls.
2. clothing.

drifter a fishing boat that floats along dragging a wide net.

drill 1. a tool for making holes.
2. exercises usually done by soldiers.

drink to swallow a liquid.

drip to fall in drops.
A tap will *drip* if it needs a new washer.

drive 1. to make a machine go.
2. a ride in a vehicle like a motor car.
3. to force along.
The dogs will *drive* the sheep to the pen.
4. the road leading to a large house.

driver 1. a person who drives.
2. a golf club for hitting the ball a long way.

drone 1. a humming or buzzing noise.
2. a male honey-bee.

drop 1. a small amount of liquid in a round shape.
2. to let something fall.

drown to die under water because there is no air to breathe.

drum 1. a hollow cylinder.
2. a musical instrument, played by beating it with the hands or with sticks.

drawbridge

drum

duck

duel

Ee

dry   without water.

duck   1. a swimming bird with a flat beak and webbed feet.
2. to bob down quickly.

duel   a fight between two people using swords or guns.

duet   a piece of music played or sung by two people.

duffel-coat   a coat made of thick, woollen cloth with a hood.

dull   1. blunt.
The sword edge was *dull* because it needed sharpening.
2. uninteresting.
John put his book away because it was *dull*.
3. not sunny.

during   while something lasts.

dusk   the time between daylight and darkness.

dust   tiny bits of powdered dirt.

dustbin   a metal or plastic container to hold rubbish.

duster   a cloth for removing dust.

dwarf   1. a tiny person.
2. any animal or plant much smaller than usual.

dwell   to live in one place.

each   every one.
Each child had a lollipop.

eager   1. wanting something very much.
2. keen to do something.

eagle   a large bird with a sharp, curved beak and talons. It kills small animals for food.

ear   1. the part of the body used for hearing.
2. the grain on a stalk of corn, such as wheat.

ear-ache   a pain in or near the ear.

early   in good time or before the time fixed.

earn   to get something, usually money, by working for it.

earrings   jewellery worn on or through the ears.

earth   1. the world where we live.
2. the ground or soil where we plant things.

earthquake   a violent shaking or splitting open of the surface of the earth.

easel   a stand to hold a blackboard or a picture which an artist is painting.

easel

east   one of the four main compass points; the opposite to west.
The sun rises in the *east*.

Easter   a holy time of year when Christians celebrate Jesus rising from the dead.

easy   simple; not hard to do or understand.

eat   to bite food and then chew and swallow it.

echo   a sound which bounces back in a building, cave or tunnel.

eclipse   the cutting off of light when the moon comes between the earth and the sun.

edge   1. the cutting part of a knife or sword.
2. the end or rim of something.
The book fell over the *edge* of the table.

eclipse

eel   a long, thin fish which looks like a snake.

egg   an oval object laid by birds and certain other animals.
Many animals live inside an *egg* until they are born.

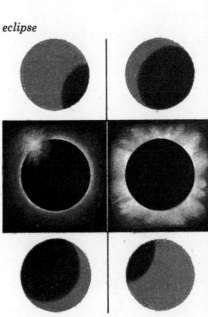

either   one or the other of two things.
You may have *either* a sweet or an apple, but not both.

eject   to throw out.

elastic   a material made from rubber which stretches and then springs back to normal size.

elbow   the joint in the middle of the arm where it bends.

elevator

lift

grain elevator

elder   1. a tree with purple berries.
2. an older person.
3. not as young as (between two).
John is 10, Fiona his sister is 14. She is the *elder*.

electricity   power used to make light and heat or drive machines.

elephant   a big animal with tusks and a long nose called a trunk.

elevator   1. a lift.
2. a building for storing grain.

elf   a very small, boy fairy.

elk   a large deer with large, flat antlers.

elm   a large tree with hard wood. Its branches spread wide and give plenty of shade.

emerald   a bright green, precious stone.

emergency   a sudden or unexpected happening which calls for quick action.

empty   1. to take everything out of something.
2. with nothing in it.

emu   a large Australian bird which cannot fly.

end   the last part of something; the finish.
The traveller came to the *end* of his journey.

enemy   someone who fights against you.

engine   a machine which makes power to do work.
A car has an *engine* to make it go.

engineer   someone who makes or repairs engines and machines.

enjoy   to like doing something.
I *enjoy* eating ice-cream.

enormous   very, very large.
The whale is an *enormous* animal.

enough   just as much as is needed and no more.

entertain   to amuse and make people happy.

entertainment   something to amuse and entertain, such as a show or a play.

emu

entrance   the way in.

envelope   a folded cover or wrapper especially for a letter.

equal   of the same size or value.
Twelve and a dozen are *equal*.

equator   an imaginary line round the centre of the earth.

errand   a short journey to do something for someone.

error   a mistake; something that is done wrongly.

escape   to get away to freedom.
The tiger was able to *escape* from its cage.

Eskimo   one of a group of people who live in North America and Greenland.

estimate   to judge the size or value from what is seen.

eve   1. the night before.
The night before Christmas is Christmas *Eve*.
2. a short way of writing evening, often used in poetry.

even   1. level; smooth.
2. a number which can be divided exactly by two.

evening   the close of day before night.

ever   at all times; always.

evergreen   a plant or tree with green leaves all the year round.

everybody/everyone   all people.

everything   all things.

everywhere   in all places.

evil   very wicked.

ewe   a female sheep.

exactly   just right.
The two jigsaw pieces fitted *exactly*.

evergreen trees

incense cedar

deodar cedar

monkey puzzle

yew

explode

eye

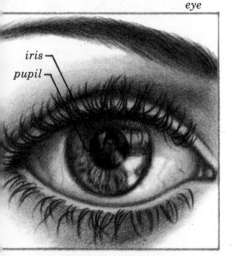

iris
pupil

examination   1. a test.
John did well in his English *examination*.
2. a careful look or search.
The doctor gave the sick boy an *examination* to find out why he was ill.

examine   to test; to look at very carefully.

example   something chosen specially as a model to copy.

excellent   very, very good.

exchange   to give one thing and get another back.

excite   to thrill or stir up strong feeling.

excitement   a very strong feeling of pleasure.

excursion   a trip or journey taken for pleasure.

excuse (as in **loose**)   a reason for not doing something.

excuse (as in **confuse**)   to forgive or pardon.

exercise   1. the training of mind or body.
2. a task to give practice.

exile   a person sent away from his home or country.

exit   the way out.

expect   to think something will happen.

explain   to make the meaning clear.

explode   to blow up or burst with a loud bang.

express   1. a very fast train.
2. to speak or write about ideas clearly.

expression   the look on a person's face.

eye   the part of the body used for seeing.

eyebrow   the hair above the eye.

eyelash   the hairs on the edge of the eyelid.

eyelid   the cover of skin used for opening or closing the eyes.

eyesight   the power to see.

Ff

fabric   cloth or any material like cloth.

face   1. the front part of the head.
2. the front of something like a clock.

fact   something that is true.

factory   a building where things are made, usually with the help of machines.

fade   to become weak, usually of colour or brightness.

fail   to try but be unable to do something.

failure   something not done properly.

faint   1. weak; dim; not clear.
2. to become unconscious from weakness.

fair   1. just; honest.
2. light in colour.
3. a place for fun with roundabouts and games.
4. a festival.

fairy   a small, imaginary person in stories.

faith   believing in someone or something.

faithful   able to be trusted; true.

fall   to drop or come down.

false   1. wrong; not true.
2. imitating the real thing.

family   people related to each other by birth or marriage; a father, mother and their children.

famine   a very great shortage of food, so that people are starving.

famous   well known for something good.

fan   1. a machine for making a cool breeze.
2. one who is very fond of sport, a hobby or a famous person.

fang   a long, pointed tooth.

far   a long way away, not near.

fare   money paid to ride on a vehicle such as a bus or train.

factory

fairy

fearless

feelers

farm   1. land where food is grown and animals kept.
2. the building where a farmer lives.

farmer   a man who works on his own farm.

farming   growing food or keeping animals for food.

fast   1. very quick.
2. fixed; unable to move.
3. to go without food.

fasten   to join together or lock.

fat   1. plump and round.
2. the soft, oily part of the body of man or animal.

father   a man who has children of his own; a male parent.

fault   anything which spoils and stops something being perfect.

favour   a kind action.

favourite   the person or thing liked best.

fawn   a young deer.

fear   a feeling of being in danger.
Some children have a *fear* of the dark.

fearless   very brave; afraid of nothing.

feast   a rich and enjoyable meal eaten at a special time.

feather   one of the pieces making up the soft coat of a bird.

February   the second month of the year. It has twenty-eight days except in a leap year when it has twenty-nine.

feeble   very weak.

feed   to give food to someone or something.

feel   1. to touch.
2. to have feeling.

feelers   the hair-like prongs on an insect's head with which it feels.

felt   a thick, woolly cloth often put underneath a carpet.

female   a woman, or animal that can have babies.

fence   wooden posts or wire joined together and put round a field or garden.

fern   a plant with feathery leaves but no flowers.

ferry   a boat to take cars or people across water.

fertile   able to produce good crops.

festival   a time for feasting, dancing and music.

fetch   to bring or carry.

fever   a sickness making the body very hot.

few   not many.
There are *few* trees in a desert.

fibre   a small thread.

field   1. a piece of land with a hedge or a fence or a wall round it.
2. a place where ball games are played.

fiend   a devil or an evil spirit.

fierce   wild; savage.
The jungle is full of *fierce* animals.

fight   to struggle with someone often using fists or weapons.

fill   to leave no space for anything more.

filly   a young female horse.

film   1. material used for taking photographs in a camera.
2. a moving picture seen in a cinema.

filthy   very dirty.

fin   part of a fish which helps it to balance and swim.

find   to see something that has been lost.

fine   1. sunny and dry.
As it was a *fine* day we went to the seaside.
2. money paid as a punishment.
3. very thin, like a thread.

fern

passenger and car ferry

fire engine

fireworks

finger   part of the hand.

fingerprints   the marks made when fingers are pressed on something.

finish   1. to end.
2. the end of a race.

fir   an evergreen tree with leaves like needles. and with cones.

fire   1. to shoot a gun.
2. something burning.

fire-engine   a vehicle specially made to carry the men who put out fires.

fireman   a man who is trained to fight fires.

fireplace   a special place for a fire to burn in.

fire-station   a building where fire engines are kept and firemen train.

firewood   small pieces of wood used to light a fire.

fireworks   small explosives made from gunpowder in a hollow tube.
Catherine wheels, roman candles and rockets are all *fireworks*.

firm   1. strong; solid.
A house is built on *firm* ground.
2. a business or company, such as the one that printed this book.

first-aid   help given immediately after an accident, until those hurt can be taken to a doctor.

fish   a swimming animal which lives in water.
A *fish* breathes through its gills.

fisherman   a man who catches fish.

fishing-boat   a boat used when catching fish.

fishing-net   a net used to catch fish.

fist   the hand with the fingers tightly pressed into the palm.

fit   1. in good health.
2. to be just the right size and shape.

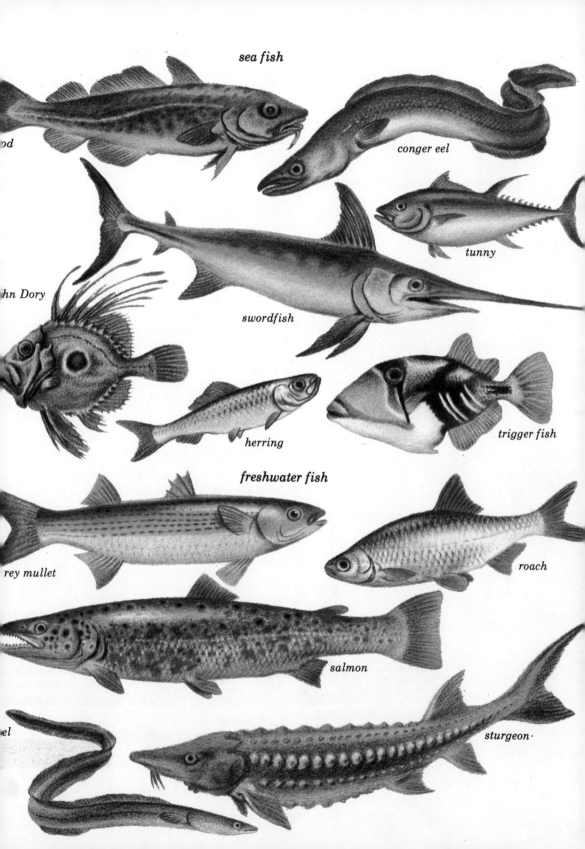

sea fish

od

conger eel

tunny

hn Dory

swordfish

herring

trigger fish

freshwater fish

rey mullet

roach

salmon

el

sturgeon

flags

Nigeria

Singapore

Sweden

Ireland

fix   1. to repair or mend something.
2. to hold steadily.
Fix your eyes on me.

flag   a piece of cloth with a special pattern.
Each country has its own *flag* with its own
special pattern.

flagon   a large bottle with a handle.

flame   a tongue of fire.

flannel   a soft woollen cloth. It is sometimes used
for washing hands and faces.

flap   1. something hanging down loosely.
2. to move up and down like a bird's wings.

flask   a flat-sided kind of bottle.

flat   1. smooth and level.
2. a set of rooms on one floor of a large
building.

flavour   the special taste of something eaten or
drunk.
A lemon's *flavour* is sharp and sour.

flee   to run away in great fear.

fleece   the woolly coat of a sheep.

fleet   1. a number of ships sailing together.
The Spanish Armada was a *fleet* of
warships.
2. a number of vehicles.

flesh   the soft parts of the body covering the
bones.

flight   a movement through the air, such as that
of a bird or aeroplane.

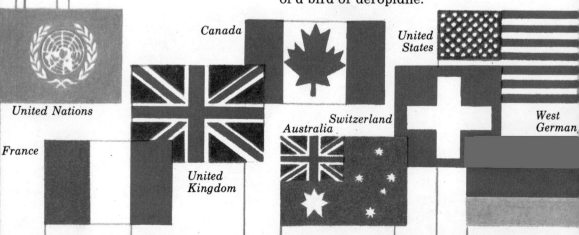

United Nations

France

Canada

United
States

United
Kingdom

Australia

Switzerland

West
German

flint　a hard kind of stone which gives off sparks when struck with steel.

flippers　1. the fins of a fish or seal.
2. rubber shoes put on the feet to help a swimmer move faster.

float　to rest on the surface of water or air.

flock　a large group of animals.

flood　an overflow of water from rivers or lakes. It may cover roads, fields and even houses.

floor　the part of a room for walking on.

florist　a person who grows or sells plants and flowers.

flour　a fine powder made by grinding grain such as wheat.

flower　the brightly coloured blossom of a plant where the seed pod is.

fly　1. to move through the air.
Most birds can *fly*.
2. a small winged insect.

fly-over　a special bridge taking one road over another road.

foal　a horse in its first year.

fog　very thick mist caused by moist dirty air.

fold　1. a place where sheep are kept.
2. to double something over; to crease.

follow　to go or come after.

food　what is eaten to keep alive.

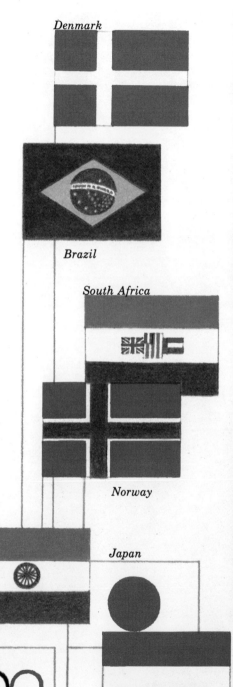

Denmark

Brazil

South Africa

Norway

China

India

Japan

New Zealand

Olympic Games

Netherlands

fort

fossil

foundry

fool   a very silly person.

foot   a part of the body at the end of the leg used for walking.

football   1. a game played by two teams.
2. a special ball for playing the game of football.
The striker kicked the *football* into the net.

footballer   a person who plays football.

footstep   the sound that the foot makes in walking.

forbid   to order that a thing must not be done.

force   1. to make someone do something.
2. a group of men such as the police force.

forecast   to say that something will happen before it actually does happen.

forehead   part of the face between the eyes and the hair.

foreign   belonging to another country; strange.

forest   a very large group of trees.

forever   going on always; never coming to an end.

forget   to let something slip out of the mind; not to remember.

forgive   to let someone off when they have done wrong; to excuse.

fork   a tool with two or three prongs used for eating or gardening.

fort   a building with high, strong walls to keep out enemies.

fortnight   two weeks; fourteen days.

fortress   a fort.

fortune   1. good or bad luck.
2. a lot of money.

fossil   the remains of a plant or animal marked in stone.

foundry   a workshop where metal things are made.

fountain   water shooting up into the air.

fowl   a bird, usually of the farmyard.

fox   a wild animal with a long, bushy tail.

fraction   a part of a whole one, like a half or quarter.

fracture   a split or crack, usually of a bone.

fragrant   sweet smelling.
The bees flew to the *fragrant* flowers.

free   1. not costing anything.
2. able to do as one likes; not a prisoner.

freedom   being free.

freeze   to turn into ice.
Water will *freeze* when it is very cold.

freezer   a machine for freezing the food which is put in it to keep it fresh.

fresh   1. new; just made; not bad.
2. not tired.

Friday   the sixth day of the week.

friend   a person one knows and likes very much.

friendly   showing liking for and kindness to someone.

fright   a sudden fear.
The hooting of an owl gave Jane a *fright*.

frighten   to make someone afraid.

frock   a dress, worn by a girl or a woman.

frog   a small web-footed animal which lives in or near water.

from   1. out of.
Steel is made *from* iron.
2. at a distance.
Hong Kong is a long way *from* Cardiff.

front   the part which faces forward; the most forward part.

frost   frozen mist or dew.

fountain

fox

frog

fruit

frown   to wrinkle the forehead to show anger.

frozen   so cold that water becomes ice.

fruit   the part of a plant or tree which holds the seeds.
The apple is the *fruit* of the apple tree.

fry   1. to cook in hot fat or oil.
2. a young fish.

fuel   anything burned to make heat.
Coal is a *fuel*, so is gas.

full   filled so that it cannot hold any more.
The jug was *full* to the brim.

fun   joy; something which makes one happy.

funny   making one laugh.
Jokes are *funny*.

fur   the soft coat of hair covering an animal's body.

furniture   things found in the rooms of a house.
Chairs, tables and beds are *furniture*.

furrow   a long, narrow groove cut into the ground by the blade of a plough.

fury   great anger.

fuselage   the body of an aeroplane.

future   the time still to come; after now.

Gg

galleon

gain   1. to collect something more by trying hard.
2. to earn or win.

galaxy   a group of stars in the sky.

gale   a strong wind.

galleon   a sailing ship with three masts.

gallery   a long room where pictures are on show.

galley   a long, narrow ship with rows of oars on each side.

gallon   a measure of liquids.

gallop   1. the fastest running pace of a horse.
2. to run heavily.

game 1. something played using a set of rules.
2. hunted animals.

gang 1. a group of workmen.
2. a group of thieves or robbers.

gap a space or opening between two things.

garage a place where cars are kept.

garden a piece of ground for growing flowers, fruit or vegetables.

gardener a person who owns or works in a garden.

garland a ring made of flowers worn round the head or round the neck.

garment a piece of clothing worn on the body.

gas something like air, not solid and not liquid. We use *gas* for heating and cooking.

gate a wooden or metal barrier. It can be moved to open or close an opening in a wall, fence or hedge.

gather to collect together into one group. A crowd began to *gather* in the market place.

gay very happy and full of life and fun.

gaze to look at very steadily for a long time.

gazelle a small, fast-running antelope.

general 1. an officer of high rank in an army.
2. belonging to or of interest to everyone.

generous ready to give things to people who need or want them.

gentle/gently not rough; with a light gentle touch. The doctor *gently* picked up the frightened child.

geography the study of the earth and the people, plants and animals on it.

germ a tiny living thing seen only under a microscope. Some germs make people ill.

garden

gazelle

gipsies

glider

ghost the spirit of a dead person which some people say comes back to earth.

giant 1. a very large person or thing.
2. huge.

gift something given; a present.

gigantic very, very big, like a giant.

gill an opening in a fish's skin used for breathing.

ginger the root of a plant grown in hot countries. It has a hot flavour.

gipsy/gypsy one of a group of people who wander from place to place, sometimes in caravans.

giraffe a large animal from Africa, with spotted skin, a long neck and long legs.

girl a child who will grow up to be a woman.

give to hand over something without charging.

glacier a slow-moving river of ice.

glad happy; full of joy.

glance 1. a quick look.
2. to bounce off at a slant.

glass 1. a hard material which can usually be seen through.
2. something made of glass, like a tumbler.
3. a mirror.

glasses another word for spectacles.
Glasses help some people to see better.

glide to move smoothly through air or water.

glider a light aeroplane with no engine.

globe 1. a round object like a ball.
2. a map of the world on a globe.

glove a covering for the hands with separate places for each finger.

glue something used to stick things together.

gnat   a small flying insect. It bites to suck blood.

gnaw   to chew and bite with the front teeth.
The rabbit began to *gnaw* a carrot.

gnome   a storybook dwarf who lives underground.
There is a plastic *gnome* in the garden.

goal   a place to aim at in a game.
Footballers try to kick the ball into the *goal*.

goat   an animal like a sheep with pointed horns and a beard.

goblin   an elf who stirs up trouble in fairy stories.

god   someone or something that is worshipped.

goggles   spectacles which fit closely to the eyes to protect them.
Skiers usually wear tinted *goggles*.

gold   a very valuable yellow metal.

goldfish   a small red or gold coloured fish often kept as a pet.

golf   a game played with a small ball and a set of sticks called clubs.

gondola   a long, narrow boat used on the canals in Venice.

gone   left; moved away.
They have *gone* to live in the United States.

good   1. well behaved.
2. of a high standard.
Joan's *good* work won a prize.

goodbye   a word said when going away.

goose   a bird like a large duck, with webbed feet and a long neck.

gooseberry   a fruit with a hairy skin.

gorilla   the largest kind of ape.
The *gorilla* lives in the forests of Africa.

gown   a woman's dress, usually long enough to reach the floor.

grab   to catch hold of something suddenly.

goggles

gondola

grapefruit

grain 1. the seeds of some plants such as corn.
2. a very small piece of something.
It is difficult to see one *grain* of salt as it is so small.
3. the lines in wood.

gram a very small weight.
1000 *grams* make 1 kilogram.

granary a building where grain is kept.

grand very large and important.

grandad/grandfather/grandpa the father of a mother or father.

grandma/grandmother/granny the mother of a mother or father.

granite a very hard rock used for building.

grape a small, round fruit which grows in bunches on a plant called a vine.

grapefruit a fruit like an orange but usually bigger and with a yellow skin and a sour taste.

grass a plant with thin, green leaves grown in fields and on lawns.

grasshopper a small jumping insect which rubs its back legs or its wings together to make a chirping noise.

grass snake a small harmless snake.

grateful full of thanks.
The hungry man was *grateful* for the meal.

gravity the pull of the earth. It makes things come down when thrown up or dropped.

gravy a sauce, usually made from the juice of cooked meat.

graze 1. to eat grass while it is still growing.
2. to rub off a piece of skin.

grease thick oil or animal fat often used to make machines work smoothly.

grape

graze

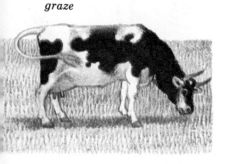

great   1. large.
      2. very important.
      King Alfred was a *great* king.

greedy   wanting more than a fair share.

green   the colour of growing grass.

greengrocer   a person who sells vegetables and fruit.

greenhouse   a glass house where plants are grown.

greet   to speak in a friendly way on meeting someone.

grey   1. the colour of a cloudy sky.
      2. a colour made by mixing black and white.

grief   deep sadness.

grip   to hold tightly.

grizzly   a big, fierce, brown bear found in North America.

grocer   a shopkeeper who sells food such as tea, sugar, butter, bacon and biscuits.

gross   1. very fat.
      2. twelve dozen (144).

ground   1. the earth that we walk on.
      2. crushed to a powder, as ground coffee.

group   a number of people or things all together.

grow   to get bigger.

growl   the sound made by an angry animal such as a dog.

grub   the form an insect has when it first hatches out of an egg; a caterpillar or maggot.

grunt   a rough, low noise as made by a pig.

guard   1. to look after or keep safe.
      2. the person who is on guard.

guess   to say or think something without real knowledge or reason.

guide   1. to show the way; to lead.
      2. the person who shows the way.

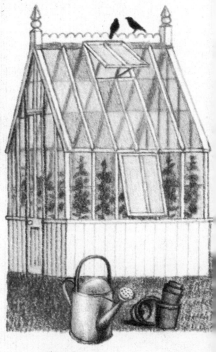

greenhouse

grocer

guitar

guilty   having done something wrong.
The robber was *guilty* of stealing the money.

guinea-pig   a small, furry animal with no tail, often kept as a pet.

guitar   a musical instrument with strings for plucking to play music.

gulf   a stretch of sea almost surrounded by land.

gum   1. the firm flesh round the teeth.
2. a kind of glue.

gun   a weapon for shooting bullets or shells.

gunpowder   a powder which explodes when lighted.

gutter   an open drain for rainwater; it is either at the side of the road or on the roof of a house.

gymnasium   a building or large room specially fitted out so that people can exercise and keep fit.

Hh

habit   a thing done so often that it is done almost without thinking.
Brushing your teeth is a good *habit*.

haddock   a large sea fish very like a cod.

hail   frozen rain.

hair   the soft threads growing on the heads and bodies of mammals.

hairdresser

hairdresser   someone who cuts and takes care of hair.

hairy   covered with thick hair.

hake   a sea fish caught for food.

half   one of two equal parts.

half-hour   thirty minutes.

hall   1. a very big room where meetings are held.
2. the entrance to a house.
3. a large building.

ham   meat from the leg of a pig.

hamburger   1. a round piece of chopped meat and cereals fried before it is eaten.
2. a sandwich made with a hamburger and roll.

hammer   a tool with a wooden or metal handle and a heavy metal head. It is used for hitting things such as nails into wood.

hammock   a swinging bed usually made of netting or canvas.

hamster   a small, furry animal often kept as a pet.

hamster

harbour

hand   the part of the body at the end of the arm.

handbag   a small bag women and girls use to hold such things as money, make-up and a handkerchief.

handicraft   making things by hand.

handkerchief   a small piece of cloth used for wiping the nose.

handle   1. the part of something held in the hand.
2. to touch something with the hands.

handlebar   the part of a bicycle held with the hands to guide it.

handsome   good-looking.

handwriting   a way of writing by hand.

hang   1. to fasten up something so that it swings freely.
2. to swing freely.

hangar   a large shed for aircraft.

happen   to take place.
Accidents can *happen* to anyone.

happiness   a feeling of being glad or full of joy.

happy   full of joy.

harbour   a sheltered place where ships are safe.

hard   1. firm like a piece of rock.
2. not easy to do.

hare   an animal like a large rabbit which can run very fast.

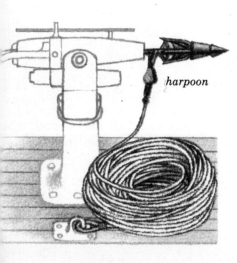

harpoon

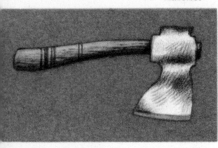

hatchet

hawk

harm   hurt; damage.

harmless   not able to hurt.

harness   the leather straps put on a horse for riding or for pulling a cart or wagon.

harpoon   a sharp spear used to kill fish or whales.

harvest   the time when the ripe crops are gathered in.

hat   a covering worn on the head.

hatch   1. to be born from an egg by breaking the shell.
2. an opening in the deck of a ship.

hatchet   a small axe.

hate   to dislike strongly.

have   to own; to hold.
We *have* ten toes.

hawk   a bird which kills small birds and animals for food.

hawthorn   a small tree with pink or white flowers and red berries.
Many hedges are made of *hawthorn*.

hay   dried grass. It is used to feed cattle and horses.

head   the main part of anything; the part of the body above the neck.

headache   a pain in the head.

headteacher   a man or woman in charge of a school and its teaching staff.

health   how the body is, whether it is fit or not.

healthy   in good health; free from illness.
Good food and exercise help to keep people *healthy*.

heap   a pile of things, like a pile of coins.

hear   to take in sounds through the ears; to be aware of sounds.
We *hear* sounds with our ears.

heart the part of the body that pumps blood round the body.

hearth the floor of the fireplace; the fireside.

heat 1. warmth.
2. to make something hot.

heater something which gives out heat, like a fire.

heavens the sky.

heavy of great weight.

hedge a row of bushes planted close together to make a fence.

hedgehog a small animal with sharp prickles on its back.

hedgehog

heel 1. the back of the foot.
2. the back of a boot or shoe.

heifer a young cow.

height 1. how tall something is.
2. the distance from the ground upwards.

helicopter an aircraft without wings lifted into the air by whirling blades.

helmet a hard kind of hat worn to protect the head.
The driver of a motorcycle must wear a *helmet*.

helicopter

help to make things easier for someone by sharing the work.
The children *help* their mother to wash the dishes.

helpful keen to help.

hem the edge of a piece of cloth where it has been turned over and stitched.

hen any female bird.

her/hers belonging to a woman or girl.
This is *her* book. It is *hers*.

herd a group of animals together, such as a herd of elephants.

here the place where you are.

helmet

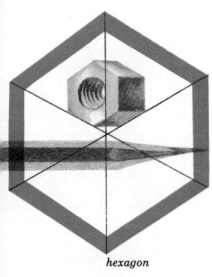

hexagon

hermit a person who lives alone, usually in a lonely place.

hero a very brave boy or man.

heroine a very brave girl or woman.

heron a long-legged wading bird which eats fish.

herring a small sea fish. When dried and smoked it is called a kipper.

hexagon a flat shape with six sides.

hidden out of sight.

hide to put or keep out of sight.

high a long way above the ground.

highway a main road.

hill a place where the ground is higher than the rest, but not as high as a mountain.

hilt the handle of a sword or a dagger.

hippopotamus a large, wild animal which lives in the rivers of Africa.

his belonging to a boy or a man.
John said the cap was *his*.

history the story of the past.

hit 1. to knock or strike something.
2. a very popular song or record.

hobby something people like to do in their spare time.

hockey a team game played with a ball and a stick curved at the end.

hoe a garden tool used for weeding and breaking ground.

hold 1. to have something in the hand.
2. the part of a ship where the cargo is kept.

hole an opening; a hollow.
The rabbit ran into a *hole* in the ground.

holiday a day when there is no work or school.

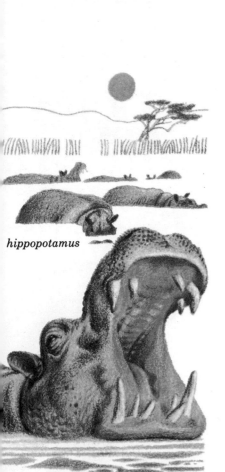

hippopotamus

hollow   empty; having a space inside.
A drum is *hollow*.

holly   an evergreen tree with prickly leaves and bright, red berries.

holy   of or belonging to God; perfectly good; godly.

home   the place where you live.

homework   school work done at home.

honest   truthful and able to be trusted.

honey   a sweet food bees make from the nectar they collect from flowers.

holly

honeycomb   the place inside a hive where bees store honey.

hood   a loose cloth covering for the head and neck. Sometimes the hood is fastened to a jacket.

honeycomb

hoof   the hard part of the foot of some animals such as the horse, cow, pig and sheep.

hook   a bent piece of metal or wood, used to catch fish or to hang things.

hope   to wish for something to happen or come true.

horizon   the place where the sky and the earth look as if they touch.

horn   1. hard bone growing out of the head of some animals.
2. a musical instrument.

horrible   most unpleasant; shocking.

horror   a feeling of fear and shock.

horse

horse   an animal used for riding or pulling carts and carriages.

horseshoe   a curved piece of metal nailed to a horse's hoof to protect it.

hospital   a building where sick or hurt people are taken care of.

hot   very, very warm.

horseshoe

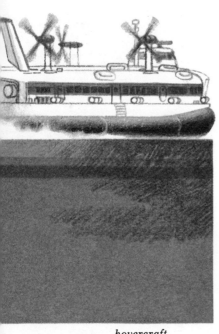

hovercraft

hot-dog a bread roll with hot sausage inside for eating.

hotel a building where people pay for a bedroom and food.

hour sixty minutes.

house a building where people live.

houseboat a floating house.

housewife a woman who does housework in her own home.

housework jobs done at home such as ironing, cooking and cleaning.

hovercraft a vehicle which glides over water or land on a cushion of air.

how in what way.
Daddy showed me *how* to mend a puncture.

howl a long, loud, wailing cry made by a dog or a wolf.

hug to put one's arms round and squeeze gently.

huge very, very big.
Whales are *huge* animals.

houses

Sumatran

European traditional

Indian tepee

Russian log hut

hull   the body or main part of a ship or boat.

humble   not full of pride; never boasting.

humming bird   a small brightly-coloured bird. Its wings flap so quickly they make a humming sound.

hungry   needing or wanting food.

hunt   1. to try to catch wild animals for fun or for food.
2. to look carefully for something.
3. a chase.

hurricane   a very bad storm with strong winds; a cyclone.

hurry   to move very quickly.

hurt   to make someone feel pain.

husband   a man who is married.

hut   a small wooden building like a shed.

hutch   a small wooden building for a pet rabbit.

hyacinth   a flower which grows from a bulb.

hyena   a wild animal with a strange laughing call. It looks like a large dog.

hymn   a song of praise to God.

hyacinth

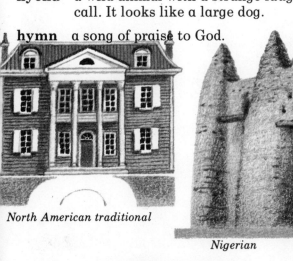

North American traditional

Nigerian

Alpine chalet

modern

Mongolian yurt

Liberian

Ii

ice

ice cubes

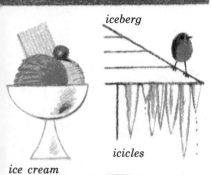

iceberg

icicles

ice cream

icing

ice   water frozen solid by the cold.

iceberg   a large piece of ice floating in the sea.

ice-cream   a food made from cream and sugar, then frozen.

ice-skate   a blade with a small edge fixed to a boot, used for gliding on ice.

icicle   a pointed spike of ice.

icing   a sweet covering put on cakes.

idea   a thought in the head.

idle   lazy; not wanting to do anything.

igloo   an Eskimo house made of blocks of snow.

ill   not well; sick.

imagine   to make a picture in the mind of what something is like.
History books help us to *imagine* life long ago.

imitate   to try to do exactly the same as somebody else; to copy.

immediately   straight away; at once.

impatient   not willing to wait.

important   having a lot of value; worth a great deal.

impossible   not able to be done.

improve   to make or become better.

inch   a measurement of length.

indoors   inside a building.

infant   a very young child.

infirmary   a place for taking care of sick or hurt people.

influenza   a very bad cold usually called flu.

information   facts given; knowledge.

inhabitant   a person who lives in a particular place.

injure   to hurt badly.

injury   a hurt; harm.
The climber who fell had a bad *injury*.

ink   a coloured liquid used for writing or printing.

inn   a building where travellers can pay for food and somewhere to sleep.

insect   a small animal with six legs.

inside   within; not outside.
Inside the parcel was a toy.

inspector   1. someone who looks at and examines things.
2. a police officer in charge of other policemen.

instalment   1. a part of a story.
2. a payment made towards the full cost of anything.

instead   in place of.
I cannot go so you must go *instead*.

instrument   1. a tool making a job easier.
2. something on which music is played.

intelligent   able to learn and remember things with understanding.

interest   a feeling of wanting to know or do something.

interesting   holding interest.

interfere   to try to stop something from going on.

interrupt   to butt in when someone is speaking or doing something.

into   going inside.
Paul went *into* the room.

introduce   to help people to know each other by telling them each other's names.

invade   to force a way into a place.

invention   something invented.
The radio was a wonderful *invention*.

inventor   a person who makes or thinks of something completely new.

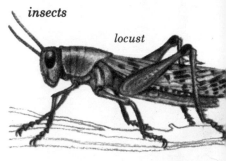

insects

locust

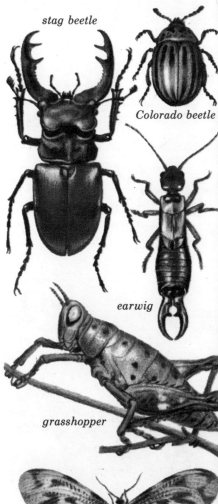

stag beetle

Colorado beetle

earwig

grasshopper

ant lion

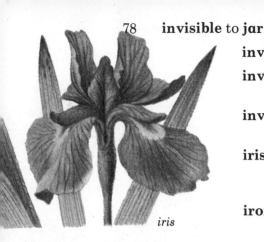

iris

ivy

ivory

invisible not able to be seen.

invitation asking someone to come to a place or to do something.

invite to ask someone to do something or go somewhere.

iris 1. the coloured part around the centre of the eye.
2. a flower with sword-shaped leaves.

iron 1. a strong, hard metal.
2. a tool, when heated, used for smoothing clothes or cloth.

island a piece of land with water all round it.

itch a tickling feeling of the skin.

it's short for 'it is'.
It's my birthday today.

its belonging to something.
The shoe has lost *its* lace.

ivory the hard, white material of an elephant's tusk.

ivy an evergreen climbing plant.

Jj

jack a tool for helping to lift heavy objects.

jackal a wild animal which looks like a dog.

jacket 1. a short coat.
2. the loose outer cover of a book.

jagged with rough, uneven edges.
The broken glass had a *jagged* edge.

jaguar an animal like a leopard living in South America.

jail a prison.

jam a sweet food made by boiling fruit and sugar until a thick liquid is formed.

January the first month of the year. It has thirty-one days.

jar a container made of pottery or glass with a very wide opening at the top.

jaguar

jaw the bone of the mouth. The teeth are fixed into it.

jealous wanting very badly something belonging to someone else.

jeans trousers like overalls made from a thick cotton cloth.

jeep a special motor car, often without a top, for driving across rough country or poor roads.

jelly 1. a sweet food made by boiling fruit juice and sugar.
Redcurrant *jelly* is eaten with roast lamb.
2. a cold, clear pudding with a fruit taste.
Mummy made a *jelly* to eat with the ice-cream.

jelly-fish a sea animal with a soft, jelly-like body. Some *jelly-fish* sting.

jerk a sudden sharp movement.

jersey a knitted long-sleeved pullover.

jet a spurt of gas or liquid coming through a narrow opening.

jet plane an aeroplane without propellers.

jewel a valuable stone, such as a diamond.

jewellery an ornament to wear, usually made of jewels and gold or silver.

jeans

jellyfish

jewellery

Greek hair ornament

Egyptian chest ornament

Peruvian mask

modern necklace

juggler

junction

jigsaw a puzzle picture made by fitting the pieces together.

job work; something that people work at.

join 1. to fasten together.
We all *join* hands to make a circle.
2. to become a member of a group, such as a choir or a club.
When I am sixteen I can *join* the Navy.

joiner someone who makes things out of wood.

joint 1. the point where two things are joined together.
2. a piece of meat.

joke something said to make people laugh.

jolly very happy.

journalist someone who writes for a newspaper or magazine.

joy a feeling of great happiness.

judge 1. a person who has to decide who is right when there is a quarrel.
2. a person who decides how someone who has done wrong should be punished.

jug a container with a handle used for pouring liquids.

juggler someone who is very clever at balancing things and keeping them moving in the air.

juice the liquid in fruit, meat and vegetables.

juicy full of juice.

July the seventh month of the year. It has thirty-one days.

jump to spring into the air with both feet off the ground.

jumper a knitted pullover with long sleeves.

junction the point where two or more things meet, such as wires, pipes, roads or railway lines.

June the sixth month of the year. It has thirty days.

jungle   land in hot countries overgrown with grass, bushes and trees.

junior   1. older than a baby but younger than an adult.
2. less important.

junk   1. rubbish.
2. a Chinese sailing ship.

just   1. fair.
A good judge gives a *just* punishment.
2. a moment ago.
She has only *just* left.
3. exactly right.
"*Just* the right amount of money," said the grocer.

junk

Kk

kangaroo   an Australian animal with strong back legs. It carries its young in a pouch on its body.

kayak   an Eskimo canoe made from bones and animal skins.

keel   the wood or metal backbone of a ship's hull.

keen   1. sharp, like a knife's edge.
2. very interested in doing something.

keep   1. to hold onto something for oneself.
2. the strongest part of a castle.

keeper   a person who looks after something, such as animals in a zoo.

kennel   a small shelter for a dog to sleep in.

kennel-maid   a girl who looks after dogs at a kennel.

kerb   the edge of the pavement.

kettle   a metal container with a handle on top and a spout. It is used for boiling water.

key   1. a piece of metal used for locking and unlocking.
2. one of the parts pressed on a typewriter or piano to make it work.

kick   to hit with the foot.

kangaroo

kayak

kilt

kites

kill   to take life away.

kilogram   a measurement of weight equal to 1000 grams.

kilometre   a measurement of distance equal to 1000 metres.

kilt   a pleated skirt usually of tartan, worn as part of the national dress of Scotland.

kind   1. friendly and helpful.
2. a sort or type of thing.

kindness   a friendly and helpful action or feeling.

king   a ruler of a country, not usually chosen by the people.

kingdom   a country ruled by a king.

kingfisher   a bird that lives by a river and eats fish.

kiosk   1. a public telephone box.
2. a small covered stall.

kipper   a herring salted and then cooked over a smoky fire.

kiss   to touch someone with the lips.

kit   all the things needed for doing a particular thing, such as football kit for football.

kitchen   the room where the cooking is done.

kite   1. a toy made of paper or cloth on a wooden frame.
2. a large bird which kills animals for food.

kitten   a young cat.

kiwi   a bird of New Zealand without wings or tail.

knee   the joint where the leg bends.

knife   a cutting tool, a flat piece of metal with a sharp edge and a handle.

knight   1. a man who has the title of 'Sir'.
2. a man who used to fight on horseback wearing armour.

knit   to weave thread into material using needles.

knitting   a knitted piece of material.

knob   1. a round handle fastened to something so that it will open more easily.
Turn the *knob* to open the door.
2. a lump.
One *knob* of butter is enough.

knock   1. to rap on something using the knuckles.
2. to hit something.

knot   1. the place where string or rope is tied.
2. a measure of speed; one sea mile per hour.
3. a mark in a piece of wood.

know   to be sure about something; to understand.

knowledge   all known things.

knuckle   a joint in a finger.

koala   a small, furry animal. It lives in the trees in Australia and carries its young in a pouch on its body.

kookaburra   a bird of Australia with a cry like a laugh.

kraal   1. South African native village.
2. a hut made of grass found in South Africa.

koala

label   a small piece of paper or cardboard fastened to a thing telling what is inside.

laboratory   a room or building where experiments in science are done.

lace   1. threadwork like a net with a pretty pattern of holes in it.
2. to tie laces.

laces   pieces of cord used to fasten things such as shoes.

ladder   steps with wooden or metal rungs fastened between two long pieces of wood or metal.

ladle   a deep spoon with a long handle used to serve soup.

lady   1. a woman
2. the wife of a nobleman.
Sir Charles is the husband of *Lady* Jane.

Ll

lace

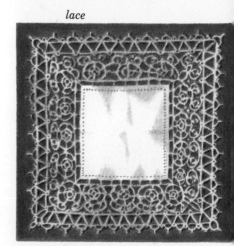

ladybird

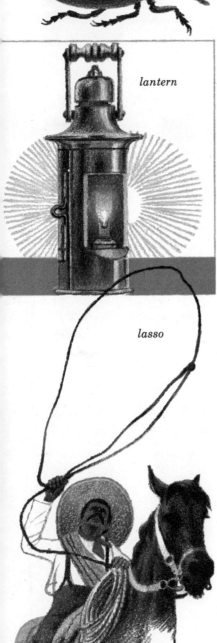

lantern

lasso

ladybird   a small flying beetle with bright spots.

lagoon   a shallow stretch of sea water separated from the sea by a sandbank.

lake   a large pond surrounded by land.

lamb   a young sheep.

lamp   a light, usually covered by glass.

lamp-post   a tall post of metal or concrete with a lamp on top.

lance   a long spear, once used by horsemen.

land   1. the ground not covered by water.
2. to come down from the air on to land or water.

landlord/landlady   a person who owns land or a house or flat and lets someone live there for money called rent.

lane   a narrow country road.

language   the words used by people when they speak or write.
Do you know another *language* besides English?

lantern   a case for holding a light. It is usually made of glass and metal.

larch   a tree with cones and long thin leaves.

lard   animal fat used for cooking.

larder   a room for keeping food.

large   very big.

lark   a small bird. It flies very high and sings sweetly.

larva   the grub of an insect.

lasso   a long rope with a sliding loop at one end, used to catch animals.

last   1. after all the rest.
2. a shape of a foot used by shoe repairers.
3. to go on for some time.

late   coming after the right time; not early.

laugh   the noise people make when they are happy or think something is very funny.

launch   1. a large motor boat.
2. to set something moving.
We watched the crew *launch* the lifeboat and rescue the seamen.

launching-pad   the place from which rockets are launched.

laundry   a place where clothes are washed, dried and ironed.

lava   the melted rock coming out of a volcano when it is erupting.

lavatory   a place where there is a water-closet (W.C.) and a washbasin.

law   a rule the government makes.

lawn   a well kept patch of grass, usually in a garden.

lawnmower   a machine for cutting grass.

lawyer   a person who has studied the law.

lay   1. to put down carefully.
2. to produce eggs.

lazy   not wanting to work.

lead (as in **feed**)   1. to go first and show the way.
2. a strap used to guide an animal.

lead (as in **fed**)   1. a heavy grey metal.
2. the part of a pencil for writing.

leaf   one of the thin, flat, green parts of a plant.

leak   a hole or crack that lets gas or liquid escape.

leap   a big jump in the air.

learn   to find out about things or how to do something.

least   the smallest, in size or value.

leaves

sycamore

larch

walnut

tropical philodendron

cypress

palm

leather   the skin of an animal specially treated so that it can be used to make things. Some shoes are made from *leather*.

leave   1. to go away from.
2. to let something stay where it is.

leek   a garden plant like an onion, with a white stem and long green leaves.

leek

left   the side opposite to right.

leg   a limb of the body used for walking.

lemon   a yellow fruit rather like an orange, but usually smaller and with a sour taste.

lemonade   a drink made of lemon juice, water and sugar.

lend   to let someone have or use something for a short time which they will give back.

length   the distance from end to end. My ruler has a *length* of 30 centimetres.

lens   a curved piece of glass used in spectacles, cameras and microscopes.

Lent   the Church season six weeks before Easter.

leopard   a large, spotted, wild animal of the cat family found in Africa and Asia.

leopard

less   not as much.
Five is *less* than seven.

let   1. to allow someone to do something.
2. to rent.

letter   1. a piece of writing put in an envelope to send to someone.
2. one of the parts of an alphabet.

letter-box   the opening in a door for a postman to push letters through.

lettuce   a garden plant with large green leaves, which can be eaten raw.

lever

level   flat and even.
A table top is *level*.

lever   a strong bar which helps to lift or move things.

liar   a person who tells lies.

library   1. a collection of books.
2. a place where books are kept.

lick   to touch something with the tongue, such as a lollipop or an ice-cream.

lid   a top to a container, which can be taken off.

lie   1. something untrue, either said or written.
2. to rest flat.

life   living or being alive.

lifeboat   a boat used at sea to save people from drowning.

lift   1. to move higher.
2. a metal box or cage for people to ride in from one floor of a building to another.

light   1. something which shines brightly.
2. not heavy; easy to lift.
3. to set on fire.

lighthouse   a tower with a bright light on top to warn ships of danger.

lightning   a very bright flash of light seen in the sky during a thunderstorm.

like   1. almost the same as something else.
A frog is *like* a toad.
2. to be fond of.
Most children *like* to play games.

lilac   a garden bush with white or purple blossom.

lily   a garden plant with a long stem and bell-shaped flowers.

limb   1. a leg or an arm.
2. the branch of a tree.

lime   1. a white powder made from limestone.
2. a green fruit like a small lemon.

limp   1. to walk unevenly.
2. not stiff; drooping.

limpet   a small shellfish which clings to rocks.

line   1. a long, thin mark.
2. a row, like a line of children.

lighthouse

lifeboat

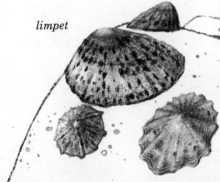

limpet

lizard

llama

lobster

linen   1. cloth made by weaving flax.
2. things such as sheets, tablecloths, towels.

linoleum   a stiff floor covering. It has a shiny surface and a cloth back.
Linoleum is often called lino for short.

lion   a large wild animal of the cat family, found in hot countries.

lip   one of the two soft edges of the mouth.

liquid   something which can be poured.

list   things written down one under another, like a list of names.

listen   to try to hear sounds with the ears.

litre   a measurement of capacity usually used to measure liquids; 1000 millilitres.

litter   1. waste paper or rubbish left lying around.
2. a number of babies born to an animal at the one time.

little   small.

live (as in **five**)   having life.

live (as in **give**)   to be alive; to make a home somewhere.

lively   full of life and energy.

liver   a part of the body for keeping the blood pure.

living-room   the room of a house where the family spend most of their time.

lizard   a reptile with four short legs and a tail.

llama   a large South American animal with a woolly coat.

load   1. something carried.
The truck carried a *load* of potatoes.
2. to prepare a gun for firing.

loaf   bread baked into a special shape.

lobster   a shellfish with two large claws.

loch   the Scottish word for a lake.

lock 1. a fastening needing a key to open it. A door has a *lock*.
2. a place on a canal or river where the level of the water can be changed to let boats sail upstream.

locomotive an engine used to pull wagons or carriages along railway lines.

locomotive

locust an insect like a grasshopper. A swarm of locusts eats up all plants in its path.

loft a room just under the roof of a building.

log 1. part of the trunk or branch of a tree after cutting.
2. the diary of the journey of a ship or aircraft.

loiter to hang around doing nothing; to go slowly.

lollipop a large sweet on a stick.

lonely feeling sad, alone, or without friends.

long far from one end to the other. It is a *long* way from Scotland to Australia.

look to turn the eyes to see something.

loom a frame on which thread is woven into cloth.

loose not fastened properly; free to move. The dog broke *loose* and ran away.

lord a ruler or master.

lorry a motor vehicle with an open platform at the back for carrying heavy loads.

lose 1. to put something where it cannot be found.
2. to be beaten in a game.

lost not to know where someone or something is; missing.

loud very noisy; easily heard.

loudspeaker an instrument for making sounds louder, so that they can be heard from a distance.

lorry

lounge 1. a room with easy chairs where people can relax.
2. to sit about in a lazy way.

love 1. to like someone very, very much.
2. the feeling of liking someone very much.

lovely beautiful.

low 1. close to the ground; not high.
2. the mooing sound made by cattle.

lower 1. to pull or let down.
The captain ordered the crew to *lower* the lifeboats.
2. not as high.

loyal faithful to friends; able to be trusted.

loyalty behaviour which shows someone can be trusted.

lumber

lumberjack

luck   something happening by chance. It can be good or bad.

lucky   having good luck.

luggage   the cases or trunks full of clothes and other things needed for a journey.

lumber   freshly cut trees.

lumberjack   a person who cuts down trees.

lump   1. a small piece of something like clay or coal.
2. a swelling or bump.

lunar   belonging to the moon.

lunch   1. the midday meal.
2. a snack or light meal of sandwiches.

lungs   the parts of the body used for breathing.

lynx   a wild cat with keen eyesight. It has tufts of hair on its ears.

Mm

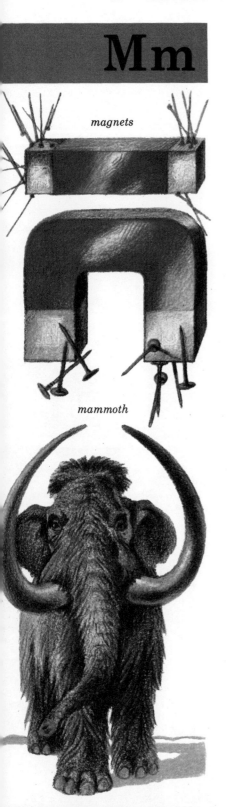

magnets

mammoth

machine a thing used to help people work more easily, such as a sewing machine.

machine-gun a gun which fires several bullets one after the other when the trigger is pressed once.

mackerel a sea fish which is good to eat.

mackintosh a raincoat; a waterproof coat.

magazine a thin book coming out once a week or once a month.

magic mysterious happenings, hard to explain, like a prince changing into a frog.

magician a person who seems to be able to make magical things happen.

magnet a piece of iron or steel with the power to pull other pieces of iron or steel towards it.

magnificent grand; wonderful to look at. A cathedral is a *magnificent* building.

magpie a large black and white bird like a crow.

maid 1. a young woman.
2. a girl or woman servant.

mail letters or parcels sent through the post.

maize a kind of corn grown in warm lands.

majesty the title of a king or queen.

major 1. an officer in the army.
2. of great importance.

make to cause; to bring into being. Boys and girls like to *make* models.

malaria an illness caused by the bite of one kind of mosquito.

malt a food made from barley and added to other foods and drinks to give richness and taste.

mammal a warm-blooded animal. The female feeds its babies with its own milk.

mammoth 1. a huge hairy elephant which lived a long time ago.
2. very big.

man   an adult male.

manager/manageress   a person who is in charge.
Everton Football Club has a *manager*.

mane   the long hair some animals, like horses,
have on their necks.

manger   an open feeding box for animals.

mansion   a very big house.

many   a lot.
A centipede has *many* legs.

Maoris   the original people of New Zealand.

Maori

map   a drawing of a place or country as it looks
from the air.
A *map* helps people find their way.

maple   a tree like the sycamore.
The *maple* leaf is the emblem of Canada.

marble   a hard stone used for fine buildings and
statues.

marbles   small round glass balls used as children's
toys.

March   the third month of the year. It has
thirty-one days.

march   to walk with steps of the same length.
Soldiers *march* on parade.

mare   a female horse.

maple

marigold   a flower with bright orange or yellow
petals.

mariner   a sailor.

margarine   a food like butter made from vegetable
oils. It is used on bread or for cooking.

mark   1. a sign showing something.
2. a spot or stain.
3. to show by sign or stain.
The pirate put an 'X' on the map to *mark*
the buried treasure.

market   a place, with stalls, where things are
bought and sold, often out in the open.

market

mask

mason

mast

marmalade   jam made with oranges, lemons or grapefruit.

marriage   a wedding; when a man and a woman become husband and wife.

marry   to become husband and wife.

marsh   soft, wet ground.

martyr   a person who dies for what he believes to be right.

marvellous   wonderful.
Television is a *marvellous* invention.

mask   a covering for the face. It can be funny or frightening.

mason   a person who carves or builds with stone.

mast   a tall pole as used on boats and ships, used for holding up sails, aerials and flags.

master   the man in charge.

mat   1. a small rug.
2. a small piece of thick material put on the table under hot dishes.

match   1. a thin piece of wood with a special tip which lights when rubbed against a rough surface.
2. a competition between two people or two teams.
3. the same in colour, shape or size.
4. to sort by size, colour or shape.

material   any stuff used for making things.
Cloth is the *material* from which clothes are made.

mathematics   the study of numbers and measurements.
Arithmetic is part of *mathematics*.

matron   a woman in charge of the nurses in a hospital.

mattress   the soft, thick part of a bed for lying on.

May   the fifth month of the year. It has thirty-one days.

may   to be possible; to be allowed to.
　　　It *may* rain today.
　　　May I have a toffee?

mayor/mayoress   the person chosen as the
　　　leader of the people in a town or city.

meadow   grassland usually surrounded by hedges
　　　or a fence.

meal   1. breakfast, lunch, tea, dinner or supper.
　　　2. ground-up corn.

mealtime   a time when food is eaten.

mean   1. selfish.
　　　2. to intend to do something.
　　　　I *mean* to work hard at school.

measles   an illness when the body is covered with
　　　small red spots.

measure   to find out the size, amount, length or
　　　weight of anything.

meat   the parts of animals used for food.
　　　Pork is *meat* from the pig.

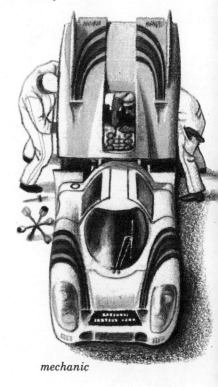

mechanic

mechanic   a person who makes or repairs
　　　machines.

medal   a piece of metal shaped like a coin or a
　　　cross given as a reward.
　　　The athlete won a *medal* at the Olympic
　　　Games.

medal

medicine   a pill or drink swallowed by a sick
　　　person to improve health.

meet   to come together.
　　　John told Ann to *meet* him at the park.

melon   a large juicy fruit. Its centre is full of
　　　seeds.

melt   to change a solid into a liquid by using heat.
　　　The sun *melts* ice into water.

memory   1. the power to remember.
　　　　His *memory* is good.
　　　2. something that we remember.
　　　　The *memory* of the holiday lasted a
　　　　long time.

mermaid

men   more than one man.

mend   to repair.
I asked mother to *mend* a hole in my sock.

merchant   a person who buys and sells things.

mercury   a heavy, silver-coloured liquid metal used in a thermometer.

mermaid   a fairy-tale woman who lives in the sea and has a fish's tail instead of legs.

merry   very happy and jolly.

mess   many things mixed up in an untidy way.

message   words sent from one person to another. A *message* can be spoken or written down.

messenger   a person who carries a message.

metal   a hard, shiny material such as iron, steel, gold, copper or silver.

metals

iron

steel

silver

gold

meteor   a shooting star.
Joan watched the *meteor* flash across the sky.

meter   an instrument for measuring.
A gas *meter* measures how much gas is burned.

metre   a measurement of length.
1000 millimetres or 100 centimetres make one *metre*.

microphone   an instrument for picking up sounds.

microscope   an instrument to make very small things look much bigger.

midday   twelve o'clock in the daytime.

middle   halfway; a spot, the same distance from each end or side.

midnight   twelve o'clock at night.

microscope

aluminium

tin

copper

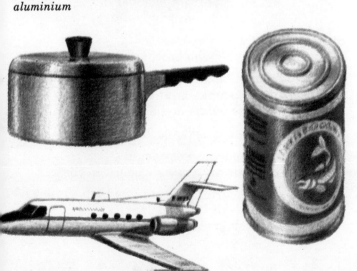

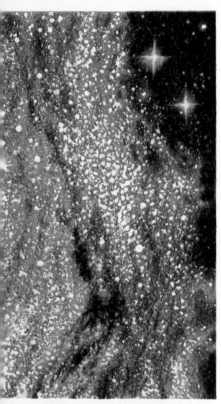

Milky Way

mill

might   1. to be possible.
It *might* stay fine even though it is cloudy.
2. great power or strength.

mile   a measurement of length.

milk   the white liquid produced by female mammals to feed their young.
We usually drink cow's *milk*.

Milky Way   a group of stars in the sky.

mill   1. a factory where cloth or steel is made.
2. a place where corn is ground into flour.

million   a thousand thousands (1 000 000).

millionaire   a very rich person.

mince   1. to chop into very small pieces.
2. meat chopped into small pieces.

mincemeat   chopped up nuts, fruit, raisins and spices used to make mince pies.

mine   1. belonging to me.
John said, "This book is *mine*."
2. a deep hole in the ground where men dig for coal, iron or other minerals.
Diamonds are also found in a *mine*.

miner   a man who works in a mine.

mineral   1. material dug out of the earth, such as rock, coal or diamonds.
2. a fizzy drink like lemonade.

minister   1. a clergyman, vicar or priest.
2. an important member of the government of a country.

minor   1. not very important.
2. a person who is still a child.

mint   1. a small, green plant with a strong taste used to make mint sauce.
2. a place where coins are made.

minute (say *minit*)   sixty seconds.

minute (say *mynewt*)   very small.
The bird was a *minute* speck in the sky.

miracle   a wonderful happening which cannot be explained.

mirror   a looking glass.

mirth   laughter; happiness.

mischief   silly things done to harm or annoy others.

miser   a person who saves all his money and lives in a very poor way when there is no need.

miserable   very unhappy.

misery   great unhappiness.

miss   1. a girl or woman who is not married.
2. fail to hit.
3. to notice when someone or something is not there.

missile   something thrown or fired. An arrow or a bullet is a *missile*.

mist   a thin fog caused by very low cloud.

mistake   something done wrongly; error.

mistletoe   an evergreen plant with white berries.

mistress   the woman in charge.

mitten   a glove with no separate place for each finger.

mix   to stir different things together.

moan   a low groaning sound made by someone who is hurt or ill.

model   1. a small but very good copy of something.
2. a man or woman who shows off clothes.

moist   damp; slightly wet. The walls of the cave were *moist*.

mole   1. a small animal which lives underground.
2. a brown spot on the skin.

moment   a very, very short time.

monastery   a place where monks live and work.

Monday   the second day of the week.

money   coins or banknotes used to buy things.

mistletoe

mitten

mole

monk

moose

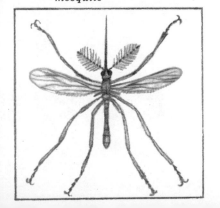
mosquito

mongrel   a dog which is a mixture of two or more kinds.

monk   a holy man.
A *monk* usually lives in a monastery.

monkey   a small, furry animal with a long tail. It is good at climbing trees.

month   a twelfth part of a year.
January is the first *month* of the year.

moon   a planet seen in the sky moving round the Earth. It looks bright because the sun shines on it.

moor   1. a large open piece of rough ground where very little grows.
2. to fasten a boat so that it will not drift away.

moose   a large animal like a deer which lives in North America.

mop   a long stick with a bundle of rags or cloth at the end for wiping floors.

more   greater than.
Five is *more* than two.

morning   the part of the day before noon or midday.

mosquito   a small, flying insect which bites.

moss   a small, spongelike plant growing on stones or trees.

most   the greatest; the largest number.

moth   an insect like a butterfly which usually flies at night.

mother   a woman who has children.

motor   an engine to make things move or work.
A motor boat, a motor cycle and a motor car are each driven by a *motor*.

motorway   a wide, safe road for motor vehicles.

mountain   a very high hill.

mouse   a small animal with sharp teeth and a long tail.

musical instruments

moustache   the hair which grows on the top lip.

mouth   1. the opening in the face for taking in food and drink, and for talking.
2. the place where a river meets the sea.

move   1. to put in another place.
2. to go to another place.

mow   to cut grass with a machine.
Father will *mow* the lawn today.

much   a lot; a great amount.

mud   a soft and sticky mixture of earth and water.

muddle   to mix up, or puzzle.

muffin   a flat cake. It is toasted before it is eaten.

mug   a large cup with straight sides and a handle.

multiply   to make something several times greater.
Multiply 4 by 3 to get 12.

mum   a short way of saying mummy.

mummy   1. a child's name for mother.
2. a dead body which has not been allowed to decay.

mumps   an illness in which the neck swells and the throat hurts.

murder   to kill someone on purpose.

murmur   1. a soft low sound.
2. to talk in a very low voice.

muscle   a part of the body, which loosens and tightens to help the body move.

museum   a building where interesting things are put on show for people to look at.
We saw armour and fossils in the *museum*.

mushroom   a small white and brown plant, shaped like an umbrella, which can be eaten.

music   1. pleasing sounds made by instruments or singing.
2. the signs on paper which people read to make tunes on instruments or by singing.

horn

oboe

grand piano   *trombone*

zither

violin

xylophone

balalaika

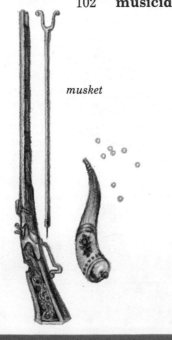

musket

Nn

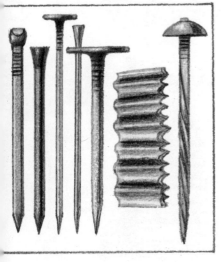

nails

musician   a person who plays a musical instrument.

musket   an old kind of gun which fired lead balls instead of bullets.

mussel   a shell fish found in the sea.

mustard   a brown or yellow paste used to flavour food, especially meat. It can be hot or sweet to taste.

mutton   the meat of a sheep.

muzzle   1. the open end of a gun.
2. the nose and jaws of an animal.
3. a covering put over an animal's face to stop it biting.

mystery   something very puzzling and difficult to explain.

nail   1. a thin, pointed piece of metal used to join two pieces of wood.
2. the horny piece at the end of a finger or a toe.

name   what someone or something is called.

narrow   not wide.
A footpath is too *narrow* for a car.

nasty   unpleasant; not good to taste.

nation   all the people in one country.

nationality   the name showing to which nation a person belongs.
John was born in Ireland so his *nationality* is Irish.

native   one who is born in a certain country.
You are a *native* of the country in which you were born.

nativity   birth.
'The *Nativity*' is the birth of Jesus Christ.

natural   just as nature made it; not made by man.

nature   all plants and animals and anything not man-made.

naughty   disobedient, badly behaved.

navigate   to steer or guide an aeroplane, ship or boat.

navy   the warships and sailors of a country.

near   close
I was so *near* the bird I could touch it.

nearly   almost.
Because I was late I *nearly* missed my bus.

neat   very tidy; everything clean and in order.

neck   the part of the body joining the head to the shoulders.

necklace   a string of jewels or beads worn round the neck as a decoration.

need   1. what someone must have.
2. to find necessary.
We *need* air to stay alive.

needle   a long, thin, pointed piece of steel used for sewing. It has a hole at one end to put the thread through.

negress   negro woman or girl.

negro   a person who belongs to the black-skinned people.

neigh   the cry of a horse.

neighbour   a person who lives near you.

nephew   the son of a brother or sister.

nervous   timid, easily frightened.

nest   a home an animal makes for its young.

net   string, thread or metal knotted or woven into a regular pattern with large or small holes. A net allows only some things to pass through the holes.

netball   a ball game between teams of seven where the ball is passed by hand and goals are scored by throwing the ball through a high hoop and net.
Netball is like basketball and is often played by schoolgirls.

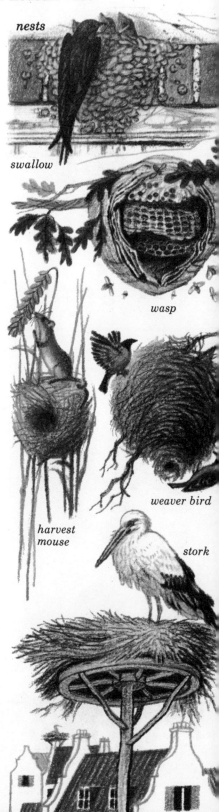

nests

swallow

wasp

weaver bird

harvest mouse

stork

newspaper

newt

nomad

never   at no time.
Never cross the road without looking.

new   fresh; just made or discovered.

news   something which has just happened.

newspaper   sheets of paper printed every day or week to tell the news.

newt   a small animal like a lizard which can live in or out of water.

next   nearest; the one following.
Thursday is the *next* day after Wednesday.

nib   the metal point of a pen where the ink meets the paper for writing.

nibble   to eat with quick, small bites.
I watched the mouse *nibble* the cheese.

nice   1. neat; very careful.
The sewing was a *nice* piece of work.
2. pleasant.

nickname   a name given or added to a proper name.

niece   the daughter of a brother or sister.

night   the time between evening and morning when the sky is dark.

nightingale   a small, singing bird found in Europe.

nimble   very quick and lively.
Monkeys are *nimble* climbers.

noble   1. splendid; fine.
2. a person of high rank.

nobody   no one at all; no person.

noise   a sound, often loud or unpleasant.

nomad   one of a group of people who wander from place to place and do not have a settled home.

nonsense   silly words and ideas, without meaning.

noon   midday; twelve o'clock in the day time.

north   one of the four main compass points; the opposite to south.

nose   the part of the face for breathing and smelling things.

nostril   one of the two openings in the nose.

not   a word which says no.

note   1. a musical sound.
2. a piece of paper money.
3. a short piece of writing.
John's mother sent a *note* to the teacher to explain his absence.

nothing   not anything.

notice   1. to see.
I *notice* that your pencil is broken.
2. a written or printed sign which tells something.

nought   the figure 0; nothing; zero.

novel   1. new and interesting.
2. a book written about imaginary people, places and events.

November   the eleventh month of the year. It has thirty days.

now   at this very moment.
Teacher said to John, "Do the work *now*, not later."

nuisance   anything which annoys or gets in the way.

number   a word or sign saying how many.
One (1) is a *number* and so is two (2).

nun   a holy woman who lives and works in a nunnery or a convent.

nursery   1. a room or building where young children play and sleep.
2. a place where flowers, trees and other plants are grown.

nut   1. a fruit or seed with a hard shell.
2. the piece of metal which screws onto a bolt.

nylon   a strong, man-made thread.

nursery

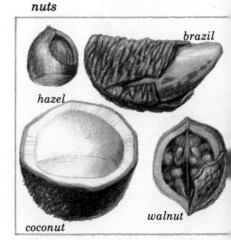

nuts

brazil

hazel

walnut

coconut

Oo

oasis

octopus

oak   a large tree with hard wood. Its fruit is the acorn.

oar   a long piece of wood with a flat end called a blade, used to row a boat.

oasis   a place in the desert where there is water, so plants and trees can grow.

oats   the grain used for making porridge.

obedient   doing as one is told.

obey   to do as one is told.

oblong   a shape longer than broad, with four square corners.

obtain   to get.

occupation   the kind of work a person does.

occur   to happen; to take place.

ocean   a large sea, such as the Pacific Ocean.

o'clock   the time by the clock.

October   the tenth month of the year. It has thirty-one days.

octopus   a sea animal with eight tentacles or arms to grab hold of its prey.

odd   1. not even; unable to be grouped in twos. Three (3) is an *odd* number.
2. strange.

off   not on.
He jumped *off* the box.

offer   1. to show or say that one is ready to do something.
2. a suggestion, sometimes giving an idea of what something is worth.

office   a place of business.

officer   a person who gives orders in the army, navy, airforce, police or fire service.

often   over and over again.

oil   a greasy liquid we take from animals or plants or from underground.

ointment   a healing paste to put on cuts and sores.

old   not new; not young.

olive   the green or purplish-brown fruit of the olive tree.

once   at one time only.

onion   a vegetable which grows in the ground in a bulb.
An *onion* has a strong taste and smell.

only   by itself; no more.

open   not shut; allowing things to pass through.

opening   a gap or hole for letting things go through.

opera   a musical play where the actors sing instead of speak.

opposite   1. face to face.
They lived in the house *opposite*.
2. as different as it possibly can be.

orange   1. a round, juicy fruit which grows in hot lands.
2. anything having the colour of the fruit.

orbit   the regular path of a planet moving round another in space.

orchard   a place where fruit trees are grown.

orchestra   a large group of musicians who play together.

orchid   a beautiful flower which usually grows in hot countries.

order   1. to tell someone to do things.
2. a list of things wanted from a shop.
3. proper position; neatness.
Write the words in alphabetical *order*.

ordinary   common and everyday; not special.

ore   a rock with metal in it, such as tin, iron and copper.

organ   1. a musical instrument with a keyboard like a piano. The sounds come from pipes.
2. a part of the body.

olive

orchid

organ

ostrich

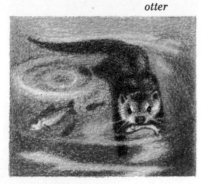

otter

oven

ornament 1. anything for adding beauty, such as jewellery.
2. a vase or a piece of pottery for decoration.

orphan someone whose parents are dead.

ostrich the largest bird in the world. It has long legs and cannot fly. It lives in parts of Africa.

other not the same one; different.

otter an animal living in or near water. It is a good swimmer and catches fish to eat.

our belonging to us.

out not in; in the open.

outback the areas of Australia far from towns and cities.

outdoors outside; in the open air.

outlaw a bad person; someone who does not keep to the law.

outside the opposite of inside; not in a building or room.

oval shaped like an egg.
A rugby ball is *oval*.

oven a closed space where food is baked by heating.

over 1. above.
The aeroplane flew low *over* the houses.
2. finished.
When the lesson is *over* the children go home.

overboard over the side of a ship into the water.

overseas in a land across the sea; abroad.

overtake to catch up and pass.

owe 1. to have to pay back something borrowed.
2. to be in debt.

owl a bird with a big head and eyes. It hunts mice, rabbits and small birds at night.

own   1. to have something that belongs to oneself.
     2. to admit.
     Will the person who broke a vase *own* up?

owner   the person to whom a thing belongs.

ox   an animal like a cow, used to pull carts.

oxygen   one of the gases in the air, needed in order to breathe and live.

oyster   a shellfish which is eaten.
     Pearls are sometimes found in *oyster* shells.

oyster

Pp

pack   1. to put things into a box, bag or case.
     2. a bundle to be carried on the back.
     3. a group of things, all the same, like a pack of cards, or a pack of animals.

package   a small parcel.

packet   a very small parcel or package.

paddle   1. to walk in shallow water.
     2. a short oar.
     3. to move a canoe using a paddle.

page   1. one side of a sheet of paper in a book or magazine.
     2. a boy messenger in an hotel.
     3. in olden days, a boy who served in a palace or lord's house before becoming a knight.

pageant   a colourful show, usually about history, with people dressed in costume.

pagoda   a temple found in the East.

pail   a bucket.

pain   an unpleasant feeling when a part of the body hurts.

painful   full of pain.
     A broken arm is *painful*.

paint   1. a coloured liquid for brushing onto a wall, wood, paper or canvas. It dries to a hard coating.
     2. to put on paint with a brush.

pagoda

panda

painting   a picture which has been painted.

pair   a set of two, like a pair of gloves.

palace   the home of a king, a queen or a bishop.

palm   1. the flat front of the hand between the fingers and the wrist.
2. a tall tree which grows in hot lands. It has large fan-like leaves at the top.

pancake   a thin, flat scone made of flour, milk and eggs. It is fried in a pan.

panda   a black and white animal like a small bear.

panda-car   a nickname given to a small police car used in Britain.

panda-crossing   a place where traffic lights hold up the traffic so that walkers can cross the road safely.

panic   fear so strong or sudden it makes a person do things without thinking.

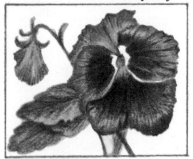
pansy

pansy   a small garden flower with three brightly coloured velvety petals.

pant   to breathe in short gasps.

panther   a kind of leopard, also called a puma.

pantomime   a musical play with a story taken from a nursery rhyme or fairy tale. We go to a *pantomime* each Christmas.

pantry   a cupboard or a small room where food is kept.

pants   another word for trousers or knickers.

paper   material used for writing, printing or drawing on. It is also used for wrapping parcels.
Paper is made from rags, straw or wood.

papyrus

papyrus   a kind of writing paper. The early Egyptians first made paper from the *papyrus* reed.

parachute   a large piece of cloth shaped like an umbrella, for floating safely down from a flying aircraft.

parade   a public march.

parallel   at the same distance apart. Two railway lines are *parallel*.

parcel   things wrapped in paper and then fastened with string or sticky tape.

parchment   the dried skin of a goat, sheep or lamb on which people used to write.

pardon   to forgive.

parent   a mother or father.

park   1. an open space in a town or city set aside for people to enjoy themselves. It usually has grass, trees and flowers and a children's playground.
2. a place to leave cars.

parliament   the meeting place of the men and women who are chosen to make the laws of a country.

parrot   a bird with bright feathers and a sharp, hooked beak. It lives in very hot lands and is often kept as a pet.

part   1. a piece.
2. to split something; to separate.

partition   1. to divide into equal parts.
2. a dividing wall.

party   a group of people having fun together. We all like a birthday *party*.

pass   1. to overtake.
2. to get through an examination.
3. to hand something to someone.
4. a narrow passage between two mountains.
5. a ticket which lets a person do something.

passenger   a person who rides in a vehicle.

passport   a special pass needed to travel to other countries.

parachute

parrot

pasture

pavement

pea

paste 1. a thick mixture for sticking things together.
2. a food spread on bread or toast.

pastime a game or hobby to pass the time happily.

pastry 1. a mixture of flour, water and fat used for baking.
2. the crust of pies or tarts.

pasture a field where cattle and sheep eat the grass.

pat to tap gently.

patch a small piece of cloth sewn over a hole or tear in clothing.

path a narrow track for walking along.

patient 1. able to wait calmly for a long time.
2. a person who is being treated by a doctor.

patrol a group of people who go back and forth keeping a look out for signs of trouble.

pattern 1. something to be copied, like a dress pattern.
2. a drawing made up of curved or straight lines used over and over again.

pavement a path of flat stones by the side of the road, where people can walk in safety.

paw the foot of an animal with claws.

pay to give money for work done, or for something bought.

pea a round green seed which we eat. It grows with others in a pod.

peace 1. quietness and calm.
Shepherds enjoy the *peace* of mountain valleys.
2. a time when there is no war.

peaceful quiet and still.

peach a juicy fruit with a soft, velvety skin. It grows in warm places.

peacock   a large bird with a beautifully coloured fan-like tail.

peak   1. the top of a hill or mountain.
2. the highest part.
3. the hard, front part of a cap.

peal   the loud sound made by bells or thunder.

peanut   a kind of nut which ripens underground. It is eaten raw or roasted.

pear   a juicy yellow or green fruit shaped like a cone.

pearl   a jewel found inside some oyster shells. The *pearl* is used to make necklaces.

peat   a substance made when plants rot in a bog. *Peat* is cut, dried, and used as a fuel for the fire.

pebble   a small round stone, often found on beaches.

peck   to bite or pick up food with a beak.

peculiar   strange; odd; unusual.

pedal   the part of a machine worked by the foot, like a bicycle pedal.

pedestrian   a person who is walking.

pedlar   a person who goes from door to door selling things.

peel   1. the outer skin of a vegetable or a fruit.
2. to take off the outer covering.

peep   to take a quick look.

peg   a wooden or metal clip used to hold things, like a clothes or tent peg.

pelican   a large fish-eating water-bird with a pouch under its beak.

pen   a tool for writing with ink.

pencil   a tool for writing. It is made of wood and has a thin strip of black or coloured material in the middle.

peacock   *peahen*

pelican

pens

pendulum

periscope

pendulum   a weight on a rod or piece of string or chain which swings backwards and forwards.

penguin   a black and white swimming-bird with webbed feet. It lives near the South Pole.

penknife   a small knife with blades which fold into the handle.

penny   a coin.

pentagon   a shape with five equal sides.

people   human beings.

pepper   1. a hot-tasting powder for flavouring food.
2. a green or red vegetable which grows in hot lands.

perch   1. a fresh-water fish.
2. a piece of wood or stick on which a bird sits or stands.

perfect   entirely good or right; with no faults.

perfume   1. any sweet smell.
2. a sweet-smelling liquid usually worn by women.

perhaps   maybe; possibly.
Perhaps it will rain today.

periscope   an instrument with mirrors, for seeing over, above, around or behind.
A submarine has a *periscope* to show what is going on above.

permission   freedom given to do something.
Tom's father gave him *permission* to stay up later than usual.

permit   a pass such as a bus pass or club membership card.

permit   to allow; to let someone do something.

person   a man, woman or child.

pet   an animal kept and taken care of at home.
My favourite *pet* is a dog.

petal   one of the coloured outer parts of a flower.

petrol   the liquid used to drive car engines. It comes from oil.

pheasant   a long-tailed game bird, hunted and eaten by human beings.

pheasant

'phone   short for telephone.

photograph   a picture taken with a camera.

pianist   a person who plays a piano.

piano   a musical instrument played by pressing keys so that hammers strike wires inside it.

pick   1. to choose.
The captain will *pick* his football team.
2. to gather, like flowers or fruit.
The girls will *pick* some flowers for you.
3. a tool with a curved blade fastened to a long handle. It is used to break rock or hard ground.

pickle   a vegetable, such as onion, cauliflower and cucumber, kept in vinegar.

picnic   a meal eaten outside, usually on an outing.

picture   a drawing, a painting or a photograph.

pier

pie   fruit or meat cooked in a case of pastry in an oven.

piece   a part of something, like a piece of cake.

pier   a long platform of wood, stone or metal, built out over water.

pig   a farm animal with a short, curly tail.
Pork and bacon come from a *pig*.

pigeon   a bird of the dove family. It is sometimes kept as a pet.
A racing *pigeon* flies long distances.

piglet   a baby pig.

pigmy   a member of a tribe of small people who live in the jungles of Africa.

pigtail   hair twisted and plaited together so that it hangs like a tail at the back of the head.

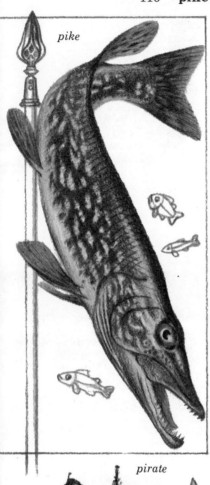

pike

pike   1. a fierce, fresh-water fish with sharp teeth.
2. a long, sharp spear.

pile   1. a lot of things heaped up together.
2. a support for a bridge.
3. the short tufts of hair on a carpet.

pill   a medicine taken in solid form.

pillar   a tall stone post. It has a round base and is used to hold up part of a building.

pillar-box   a box for posting letters. It is shaped like a pillar, and has an opening near the top for the letters.

pillow   a bag filled with soft material for resting the head on in bed.

pilot   1. a person who steers an aeroplane.
2. a person who guides a ship into port.

pin   a thin piece of metal with a small head at one end and a point at the other. It is used to fasten things together.

pinafore   an apron or overall to keep clothes clean.

pinch   1. a small amount.
She put a *pinch* of salt in the water for cooking the vegetables.
2. to nip.

pine   a tree with evergreen leaves shaped like needles and with cones.

pineapple   a large, sweet-tasting fruit which grows in hot countries.

pink   a very pale red colour.

pioneer   1. a person who does something before anybody else has thought of it.
2. a person who is the first to go and live in a new country.

pipe   1. a hollow tube to carry gas or a liquid from one place to another.
2. a tube ending in a bowl used for smoking tobacco.

pirate   a robber who steals from ships at sea.

pirate

pistol a small gun which can be fired when held in one hand.

pistol

pit 1. a hole in the ground.
2. a coal mine.

pitch 1. tar used for road-making.
2. ground on which a game is played.
3. to throw.
4. to set up a tent.

pitcher 1. the person who throws the ball in baseball.
2. a large jug.

pitcher

pity a feeling of sadness for someone in trouble.

place a particular spot; the position where something is.
Put that chair in its proper *place*!

plaice a flat sea fish.

plan 1. a drawing showing what a thing looks like from above.
2. to think out how to do something.
3. an idea for something to do.

plane 1. a tool for smoothing wood.
2. a short way of saying aeroplane.
3. a type of tree.

planet one of the large solid masses, like the Earth, which goes round the sun.

plank a long, flat, thick piece of wood.

plant 1. anything which grows in soil.
2. to place something in the ground to grow.

plastic a man-made material, used to make many things such as toys, buckets and cups.

Plasticine a soft material used for making models.

plate a flat dish for putting food on.

platform 1. a raised floor in a hall, a stage.
2. the part in a railway station where people wait for a train.

platform

play 1. a story which is acted.
2. to enjoy oneself; to have fun.

playground

plough

playground a special place for playing.
We have a *playground* at school.

playtime the time for play instead of work.

pleasant enjoyable; pleasing.

please 1. to make someone very happy.
2. the word used to ask politely for something.

pleasure happiness; feeling very glad.

plenty a supply which is more than enough.

plimsolls light canvas shoes with rubber soles worn when playing games.

plough a farm tool with a sharp, heavy blade to cut and turn over the ground. It is pulled by a tractor or in some countries by horses or oxen.

plug 1. a stopper to fill up a hole.
2. something which fits into a socket to switch on things such as an electric kettle or an electric fire.

plum a juicy, soft fruit with a hard stone inside.

plumber a man who fits and mends water pipes.

plunge to dive, or throw oneself into water.

plus added to.
4 *plus* 3 equals 7.

poacher a person who catches animals on someone else's land without permission.

pocket a small bag sewn into clothes to hold things.

pod a seed case.

poem a piece of writing where the lines usually either rhyme or have a beat or rhythm.

point 1. the sharp end of something like a needle.
2. to show something using a finger.
3. part of the score in a game.
4. a dot.

poison something which causes illness or death when taken into the body.

police

polar   of or belonging to the North or South Poles.

polar bear   a large, fierce, white-furred bear. It lives in the cold lands of the north.

police   men and women whose job it is to see that the law is not broken, or catch people who break the law.

policeman   a man who belongs to the police force.

policewoman   a woman who belongs to the police force.

polish   1. a powder or paste or liquid put on things for shining and protecting them.
2. to make something smooth and shiny by rubbing.

polite   with good manners.

pollen   a fine dust found in flowers which makes the seeds grow.

polythene   a colourless plastic material. Many goods are packed in bags made of *polythene*.

pomegranate   a round, orange-coloured fruit which is full of seeds. It grows in hot lands.

poncho   an outer garment like a cape. It is square in shape with a hole to put the head through.

pond   a small lake.

pony   a small horse.

pool   a small pond.

poor   1. having very little money or goods.
2. badly done.
This work is *poor*, I shall not accept it.

poppy   a flower usually with bright red petals.

popular   liked by a lot of people.

pork   the meat from a pig.

porpoise   a sea mammal like a small whale.

porridge   a breakfast food made from oats.

port-hole

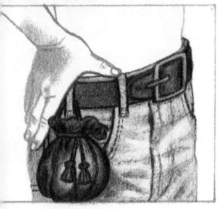

pouch

poultry

port 1. a harbour; a harbour town.
2. a drink made from grapes.
3. the left hand side of a ship or aeroplane.

porter a person who carries luggage at a station, hotel or airport.

port-hole a round window in the side of a ship.

post 1. a piece of wood or other material fixed upright in the ground.
A goal *post* is painted white.
2. letters and parcels delivered by the post office.
I've got a letter in this morning's *post*.
3. to send letters or parcels by *post*.

postcard a rectangular piece of card on which to write messages.
A *postcard* may have a picture on one side.

poster a large notice or picture put up to tell people what is going to happen.

postman the person who collects and delivers the post.

post office the place to buy stamps and to post letters and parcels. Licences of all kinds are also sold there.

potato a root vegetable which grows underground. It can be eaten when cooked.

pottery cups, vases, plates, jugs and ornaments made from clay.

pouch a small bag or sack.

poultry birds such as ducks, hens and geese kept for their meat and eggs.

pound 1. to hit very hard, again and again.
2. a piece of paper money.
3. a measure of weight.

pour 1. to make a liquid run out in a steady stream.
Will you *pour* me a glass of milk?
2. to rain heavily.

powder   very tiny bits of something, as fine as dust.
Flour is a *powder*.

pram   a small carriage for babies and young children.

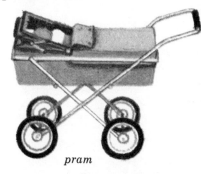
pram

prawn   a shellfish like a large shrimp.

pray   to talk to God.

prayer   the words used when people pray.

precious   worth a lot; valuable.

precipice   a very steep, high cliff.

prawn
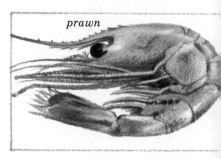

prehistoric   belonging to a time before history was written down.

present   1. a gift.
2. the present time; now.
3. here; not absent.

president   the most important person of a government, a business or a club.
The United States has a *president*.

precipice

press   1. to push steadily.
2. to smooth or flatten.
He will *press* his trousers with a hot iron after they have been washed.
3. a machine for printing such as a printing *press*.

pretend   to make believe.

pretty   attractive; pleasing.

prevent   to stop something happening.

prey   an animal hunted and eaten by other animals.

price   the sum of money needed to buy something; the cost.

prick   to make a hole with something sharp and pointed, like a needle.

primary   first of all; most important.

primrose   a yellow, wild flower which grows in spring.

prince   the son of a king or queen.

primrose

printer

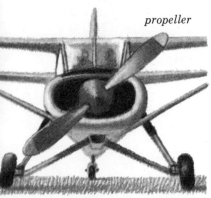

propeller

puffin

princess   the daughter of a king or queen.

print   to press letters on paper using a machine.

printer   a person who works a printing machine.

printing   writing words using separate letters like those in a book.

prison   the place where people who have broken the law are kept.

private   1. not public; secret.
2. the lowest rank of soldier.

prize   a reward which is won by people who have done something well.

problem   something difficult or confusing.

programme   1. a list of things to be seen or heard at a concert or a play.
2. a plan.
3. a show or other item on radio or television.

promise   to give ones word.

prop   to support by putting something underneath.

propeller   the turning blades which drive an aeroplane or ship.

proper   right; correct; as it should be.

properly   in the correct way.

proverb   a traditional saying.

prune   a dried plum.

pudding   a soft, cooked food usually eaten after the main course.

puddle   a small pool of water which usually dries up if it is sunny.

puffin   a sea bird found in the Atlantic. It has a short, thick beak.

pull   to draw, drag or tug something.

pullover   a knitted article of clothing pulled over the head; a jersey.

pump 1. a machine for forcing air or liquids along or up a pipe.
2. an instrument for blowing up tyres.

pumpkin

pumpkin a large yellow fruit. It grows on a vine on the ground.

punch to hit hard with the fist.

puncture 1. to make a hole in something.
2. a small hole in a bicycle or motor car tyre.

punish to make someone suffer for doing something wrong.

pupil 1. a child in school.
2. the middle of the eye, the part through which one sees.

puppet 1. a doll made to move by pulling wires or strings.
2. a doll put on the hand to make it move.

puppet

puppy a young dog.

purple a colour made by mixing blue and red.

purse a small bag or case for holding money.

push to move something by pressing hard against it.

pushchair a small pram like a chair.
A young child rides in a *pushchair*.

put to place.

putty a special paste used as cement to fix panes of glass.

puzzle a difficult problem; it may be a game like a crossword or a jigsaw puzzle.

pyjamas a loose jacket and trousers worn in bed.

pyramid 1. a shape with a square bottom and four sides like triangles meeting in a point.
2. an Egyptian monument shaped like a pyramid.

python a large snake which kills its prey by squeezing it to death.

pyramid

Qq

queue

quoits

quack the noise made by a duck.

quaint odd in an interesting and amusing way.

quantity the amount or size of something. Father ordered a large *quantity* of soil for the garden.

quarrel to disagree with someone and argue angrily.

quarry 1. a place where stone for building is dug out.
2. a hunted animal.

quarter a fourth part of anything.

quay a landing place where ships and boats can be unloaded.

queen the wife of a king or the ruler of a country.

queer strange; different from usual.

question something asked which needs an answer.

queue a line of people or vehicles waiting their turn to move.

quick very fast; lively.

quickly very soon; as fast as one can. The shop shuts soon, so go *quickly*.

quiet making no noise; still.

quilt a top covering for a bed. It is usually padded.

quit to give up; leave.

quite 1. wholly; completely.
2. just about; rather.

quiver 1. a case for holding arrows.
2. to tremble or shiver very quickly.

quiz a number of questions usually in a test, to find out how much someone knows.

quoits a game in which flat rings are thrown onto a peg.

rabbit a small animal with soft fur and long ears. The wild *rabbit* lives in a burrow.

race 1. a competition where a person tries to do something better or faster than the others.
2. to try to beat someone in a competition, usually for speed.
3. a large group of people who look alike in colour and hair, and come from the same part of the world.

rack a frame for holding things. It can have bars, pegs or shelves.

radar a way of guiding ships and aircraft using radio waves, especially at night or in fog.

radiator 1. part of a car. It cools the water that stops the engine getting too hot.
2. a set of hot water pipes joined together to heat a room.
3. an electric heater.

radio an instrument for sending and receiving sounds through the air, using electricity.

radish a red or white vegetable which grows in the ground and is eaten raw.

radium a material taken from pitchblende, used in hospitals to heal people.

raffia strips of palm leaves, usually woven into mats and baskets.

raft a platform, usually of logs fastened together, for floating on water.

rag a torn or old piece of cloth.

rage great anger.

ragged badly torn.
The beggar wore *ragged* clothing.

raid a sudden surprise attack.

rail a bar of metal or wood.
Mother bought a new *rail* for the curtains.

railing a fence made with rails.

railway the track of rails on which trains and engines run.

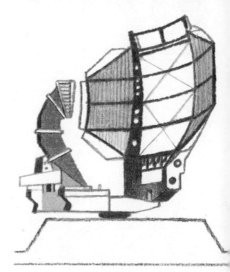

Rr

radar

raft

rainbow

rapids

rain   drops of water which fall from the clouds.

rainbow   the arch of seven colours seen in the sky when the sun shines through light rain.
The colours of the *rainbow* are red, orange, yellow, green, blue, indigo and violet.

raincoat   a long, waterproof coat.

raise   to lift up.

raisin   a dried grape.

rake   a garden tool with a long handle and a row of metal teeth like a comb.

ram   1. a male sheep.
2. to crash into something.
3. a thick, strong piece of wood used to smash down doors and walls.

ranch   a large cattle, horse or sheep farm, generally found on the prairies of the U.S.A.

range   1. the distance a weapon, such as a gun, can shoot.
2. a row of mountains.

ranger   a person who looks after a forest, a large park or a game reserve.

rapid   very quick; swift.

rapids   a place where a river flows fast over rocks and large stones.

rapier   a long, thin sword with a sharp point but no cutting edge.

rascal   someone who cannot be trusted.

raspberry   a small, red fruit with many seeds.

rat   a long-tailed animal. It looks like a large mouse and has sharp teeth.

rattle   1. a toy which makes a noise when it is shaken.
2. a short, sharp, shaking sound.

rattlesnake   a poisonous snake of America. Its tail has loose, bony rings which rattle as it moves.

raven   a large, shiny, black bird.

ravine   a deep, narrow valley made by a river wearing away the earth and stone.

raw   1. uncooked.
2. sore and red.

ray   a thin line of light, like the rays of the sun.

razor   a tool with a sharp blade used in shaving.

reach   1. to get to.
It took an hour to *reach* the zoo.
2. to stretch out the hand to touch something.

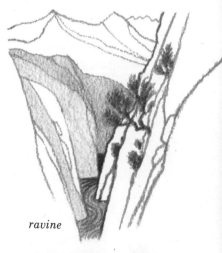

ravine

read   1. to look at words and understand their meaning.
2. to say aloud written or printed words.

reading   1. a piece of writing to be read.
2. saying the written words to oneself or aloud.

record-player

real   true; not false.

reap   to cut down and gather crops.

reason   why a thing is done or said.
I had to give a *reason* for being late.

rebel   1. a person who fights against his own country or leader.
2. to go against one's leader.

receive   to be given something.

recipe   the instructions for making something to eat or drink and what to put in it.

recorder

recite   to say aloud something learned by heart, such as a poem.

record   1. a disc played on a record-player.
2. a piece of writing about the past.
3. the very best performance.
The runner set up a new world *record*.

recorder   a musical instrument played by blowing.

record-player   a machine for playing records.

referee

rectangle   a four-sided shape with square corners. It has two equal long sides and two equal short sides.

red   a bright colour like fire.
Red usually means danger.

reed   a tall grass with a hollow stem. It grows in or near water.

reef   rocks or sand just below the surface of the sea, which are dangerous to ships.

reel   1. a lively dance.
2. a round piece of wood or metal to carry thread or wire.
Thread is often wound round a *reel*.

referee   a person who sees that the rules of a game are followed by the players.

reflect   to throw back light or heat; to mirror.

refrigerator   a special ice-box for keeping food cold and fresh.

refrigerator

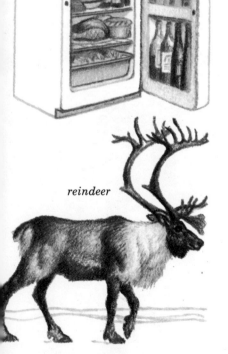

refuse   to say one will not do something.

refuse   rubbish; waste material.

register   1. a list of names or things, usually in a book.
2. to give one's name when signing something or staying at a hotel.

reign   the length of time a king or queen rules.

rein   1. one of the leather straps used to guide a horse.
2. to stop or slow down by using a rein.

reindeer   a large deer with antlers. It lives in the cold lands of the north.

rejoice   to be glad and full of joy.

reindeer

remain   1. to stay in the same place.
2. to be left behind.

remember   to store in the memory so as not to forget.

remove   1. to take away to another place.
2. to take off.

rent   1. the money paid to use something which belongs to someone else.
2. to have the use of something in return for payment.
Some people *rent* a house or a car.

repair   to mend or put right.

repeat   to say or do something again.
Please *repeat* the question. I did not hear the first time.

replace   1. to put back in place.
Replace the brush when you have used it.
2. to give something instead.
The shopkeeper agreed to *replace* the faulty machine.

reply   to answer.

report   1. to tell or write about something that has happened.
2. the loud noise of gunfire.

reporter   a person who reports things which have happened, especially for a newspaper, radio and television.

reptile   a creature such as a snake or a lizard which has cold blood and a body covered with scaly skin.

repulsive   very ugly.

rescue   to save someone who is in danger.

reservoir   a place where drinking water is stored.

rest   1. to be still and do no work.
2. a pause.
3. the others, whoever or whatever is left.

restaurant   a place where meals are served.

result   how a thing ends.
Peter lost his money. As a *result* he had to walk home.
The *result* of the match was a draw.

retreat   to go back.
The beaten army began to *retreat*.

reservoir

restaurant

rhinoceros

rice

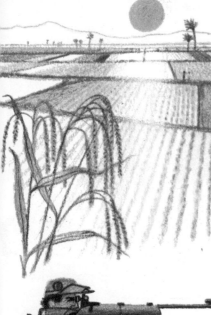

rifle

return   1. to come back to a place.
      2. to give something back.

revolver   a hand gun. It can be fired several times before it is reloaded.

reward   a present or prize given for doing well.

rhinoceros   a large African or Indian wild animal with a thick skin.

rhubarb   a garden plant. The thick, red stalks are cooked with sugar and eaten.

rhyme   1. to have the same sound as another word, such as tall and small.
      2. a piece of poetry with lines which end in words with the same sounds, like a nursery rhyme.

rhythm   a steady pattern of sound or movement. Music and poetry have *rhythm*.

rib   one of the curved bones in the chest which protect the heart and other organs.

ribbon   a long narrow strip of fine cloth used to decorate clothes or keep the hair tidy.

rice   a white grain food. It is cooked before it is eaten.

rich   having a lot of money or goods.

riddle   a puzzle, usually in words.

ride   to sit or stand on something and be carried along.

rider   a person who rides, usually on an animal.

rifle   a long hand gun. It has a groove in the barrel to make the bullet spin when it is fired.

right   1. correct.
      2. the opposite side to left.

rim   the edge of things like wheels or cups.

ring   1. a circle.
      2. a circle of metal worn on the finger.
      3. the sound of a bell.

ring-road   a special road built to go round a busy city or town.

rip   1. a long tear.
2. to tear something.

ripe   ready to use or eat, such as fruit at its best.

ripple   a small wave on the surface of the water.

rise   1. to go up in the air.
2. to get up from bed.
3. more money, usually in a person's wages.

risk   a chance, often dangerous.

river   a large stream of water moving towards a lake or the sea.

road   a hard, level track specially made for vehicles to travel along.

roam   to wander or travel about.

roar   a loud noise made by wild animals like lions.

roast   to cook meat in an oven or over an open fire.

robber   a person who steals.

robbery   the act of stealing.

robe   a long, flowing garment reaching the ankles.

robin   a small garden bird with a red breast.

rock   1. a large stone.
2. to move backwards and forwards or from side to side.

rocket   1. a firework which shoots up into the air.
2. a flying machine shaped like a tube. An astronaut is shot into space in a *rocket*.

rocky   covered with rocks.

rod   a long, thin bar of wood or metal.

rodent   an animal like a rat or squirrel. It uses its sharp front teeth to gnaw.

rodeo   a show where cowboys rope cattle and ride wild horses or bulls.

rodeo

road-roller

rose

roundabout

rogue a rascal; someone who cannot be trusted; a cheat.

roll 1. to move by turning over and over like a ball.
2. a list of names.
Is anyone missing? I'll call the *roll*.
3. a kind of bread made from small pieces of dough.

roller 1. a heavy machine rolled along to make things flat and smooth.
2. a kind of hair curler.

roof the top covering of a house, a building or a vehicle.

rook a large black bird with a hoarse, loud cry.

room 1. one part of a building, such as a bedroom or a kitchen.
2. space to put something.

root the part of a plant under the ground holding the plant firm and collecting food from the soil.

rope a thick, strong line or cord made by twisting thinner cords together.

rose a sweet-smelling flower with a thorny stem growing wild and in gardens.

rosy pinkish red in colour.

rot to go bad.

rotten bad; decayed; spoiled.

rough 1. uneven, lumpy, not smooth.
2. wild, stormy, like the sea on a rough day.

round 1. shaped like a ball.
2. the length of time boxers or wrestlers fight before they rest.

roundabout 1. a fairground merry-go-round with toy horses, cars and other things for children to ride.
2. an island built at the centre of busy crossroads for traffic to go round.

rounders   a game played with a bat and a ball. To score the batter has to hit the ball and run round four bases marked by posts, while the ball is being fielded.

row (as in **cow**)   an angry argument.

row (as in **toe**)   1. a line of things or people.
2. to move a boat through water using two oars at the same time.

rowing boat   a boat moved through water using oars.

royal   of or belonging to a king or queen.

rub   to wipe hard usually with a cloth or a brush.

rubber   1. the sap of the rubber tree and the material made from it.
Rubber can stretch and bounce.
2. a soft piece of this material used for erasing pencil marks on paper.

rubbish   1. things of no further use; litter.
2. nonsense.

rudder   a movable piece of wood or metal used to steer a boat or aeroplane.

rude   1. bad-mannered; not polite.
2. rough.

rugby   a game played using an oval ball; the players can either run with the ball or kick it. Points are given for tries or goals.

ruler   1. a piece of wood or metal used for measuring.
2. a man or woman who is the leader of a country.

run   to move quickly.

rung   one of the bars or steps on a ladder.

runway   the track laid at an airfield so that aeroplanes can land and take off.

rush   1. a tall grass growing in or near water.
2. to do something too quickly.
3. to hurry from one place to another.

rowing boat

rugby

rust   a reddish-brown coating found on iron or steel if it is left wet or damp.

rustle   a soft, whispering sound like the sound of sheets of paper being rubbed together.

rut   the deep groove left by a wheel in soft ground.

rye   a kind of grain. It is ground into flour to make ryebread.

Ss

sack   a large, strong bag made of cloth, thick paper or plastic.

sad   feeling sorry; unhappy.

safari

saddle   a seat for the rider of a horse or bicycle.

safari   a journey on foot or in cars to hunt or see wild animals.

safari park   a large area of land where wild animals are collected together so that they can be seen by visitors. In a *safari park* may be seen elephants, lions, antelopes and monkeys.

safe   1. out of danger; free from harm.
2. a very strong metal box for keeping money locked away safely.

sail   1. a sheet of cloth fixed to a ship's mast to catch the wind and drive the ship along.
2. to steer a boat.
3. to travel by boat; to float through the air.

sailor   a man who works on ships.

saint   a very good and holy person.

salad   a mixture of vegetables which is eaten cold. Lettuce, tomatoes and cress are often used in a *salad*.

sale   1. the selling of goods for money.
2. the time when shops sell goods cheaper than usual.

salmon   a large fish with pink flesh.

salt   a white powder found in the earth and in sea water; a flavouring for food.
Salt is used in cooking and at meals.

same   not different; exactly alike.
His boat is the *same* as mine.

sampan   a small boat with a flat bottom, found in countries of the east, like China and Malaysia.

sand   very small grains of rocks and shells that make up beaches.

sandal   a light, open shoe, held on the foot by straps.

sandwich   two pieces of bread with meat or some other food between them.

sap   the juice or liquid found in a living tree or plant.

sardine   a small sea fish of the herring family, often sold in tins.

satchel   a bag, used for carrying school books.

satellite   1. a planet which goes round and round a larger planet.
The moon is a *satellite* of the Earth.
2. a man-made object, such as Sputnik, that travels in space round the Earth.

Saturday   the seventh day of the week.

sauce   a liquid served with food to add to the taste.

saucepan   a cooking pot with a lid and long handle.

saucer   a small curved plate used under a cup.

sausage   a food; a meaty mixture usually put into a thin skin.

save   1. to keep something to use later.
2. to make safe; to help someone in danger; to rescue.

saw   a tool with a sharp-toothed edge used for cutting.

sawdust   the dust made by sawing wood.

say   to speak.

scald   to burn with steam or a very hot liquid.

sampan

saws

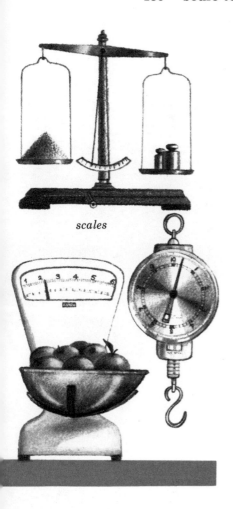

scales

scooter

scale 1. a set of musical sounds going up or down in order.
2. one of the thin, hard discs that cover the skin of some fishes and snakes.

scales a machine used for weighing and balancing.

scar the mark left on the skin after a cut, burn or sore has healed.

scarce not plentiful; hard to find.

scare to frighten.

scarf a long piece of cloth worn round the neck to keep it warm.

scarlet bright red.

scatter to throw around in several directions.

scene 1. a view; a picture.
2. a part of a play.
3. the place where something happened.

scent 1. a smell.
2. a liquid with a sweet, pleasant smell, such as perfume.

scholar a person who learns; a very clever person.

school a place for teaching and learning.

schooner a large sailing ship.

science a study of anything to do with the Earth and its surroundings by looking and testing very carefully.

scientist a person who finds out by careful testing and study why things happen.

scissors a tool used for cutting, which has two sharp blades fixed together in the middle.

scooter 1. a small, two-wheeled vehicle moved by a petrol engine.
2. a two-wheeled child's toy ridden with one foot on and one foot pushing.

scorch to burn slightly.

score 1. the number of points, goals or runs made in a game.
2. to win a point in a game.
Sally did well to *score* five goals in the netball match.
3. to keep count of the number of points in a game.
4. twenty (20).

scorpion an insect like a large spider.
A *scorpion* can push out poison from the tip of its long tail.

scorpion

scout 1. a person sent to find out what the enemy is doing.
2. a member of the Boy Scouts.

scramble to move over uneven ground using the hands and feet.

scrap 1. a small piece of something.
2. rubbish thrown away.
3. a fight.

scrape 1. to take something off with a sharp or rough edge.
Dad had to *scrape* off the loose paint before he put on the new paint.
2. trouble; difficulty.

sculptor

scratch 1. a mark made with something sharp or pointed.
2. to rub at something that itches.

scream a loud, shrill cry of fear, pain or surprise.

screw a nail with grooves used for fastening pieces of wood together.
A screwdriver twists or turns a *screw*.

scribble to write in an untidy way.

scrub to rub clean with a brush often with soap and water.

sculptor someone who shapes or carves things from stone, wood or other materials.

sea the salt water that covers about three-quarters of the earth.

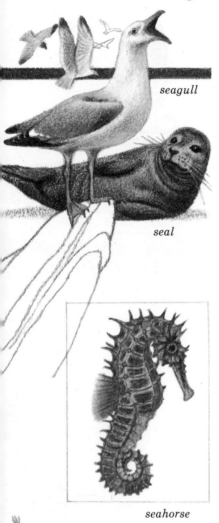

seagull

seal

seahorse

seesaw

seagull a large, white and grey sea bird that makes a loud screeching noise.

seahorse a small sea animal with a tail. Its tail helps it to swim in an upright position.

seal 1. a large sea animal. It lives both in the sea and on land and eats fish.
2. to fasten something so that it cannot be opened without breaking the fastening.

search to try to find by looking carefully.

seaside the land along the edge of the sea.

season 1. a period of time, usually part of a year, like the football or cricket season.
Spring is the first season of the year. The others are summer, autumn and winter.
2. to give more taste to food by adding salt and pepper or herbs.

seat something to sit on.

seaweed plants growing in the sea.

second 1. next after first.
Susan came *second* in the race.
2. a very short period of time.
A *second* is the sixtieth part of a minute.

secret 1. something known to only one or two people.
2. hidden.
The man escaped through a *secret* door.

see to use the eyes to look at something; to notice.

seed the part of a plant from which a new plant will grow.

seek to look for.

seem to appear to be.
You *seem* unhappy today, Ann.

seesaw a plank fastened in the middle to a strong piece of wood or metal. A person sits on each end and first one end of the plank goes up in the air and then the other.

seldom   not often; only a few times.

selfish   thinking too much of oneself; not caring for others.

sell   to give something for money.

send   to make a person or thing go somewhere.

sensible   wise.
   Mary is a *sensible* girl. She doesn't dash across the road.

sentence   a group of words that mean something.

sentry   a soldier who keeps guard.

separate   1. not joined together; apart.
   2. to go away from each other; to part.

September   the ninth month of the year.
   September has thirty days.

sergeant   a person in charge of a group of people in the army, air-force or police.
   A *sergeant* wears three stripes on each sleeve.

sentry

sergeant

serial   a story, play or film read, told, or shown one part at a time.

serious   important; not joking.

serpent   another name for a snake.

servant   someone who is paid to work for someone else, often in a house.

serve   1. to work for someone.
   2. to sell things in a store.
   3. to give people food at table.
   4. to play the first stroke in tennis.

settee   a long, soft seat, with a back, for two or more people.

several   a small number; more than two or three but not many.

sew   to use a needle and thread to join cloth together.

shabby   nearly worn out.
   The tramp's clothes were *shabby*.

settee

sew

shamrock

shark

shearing

shade
1. to keep the light away from something.
2. a cover for a light.
3. a place hidden from the sun or from the light and heat.
Meg sat in the *shade* under an umbrella.

shadow   the dark shape made by an object or person coming between the light and the ground or wall.

shake   to move anything quickly from side to side or up and down.

shallow   not deep.

shame   an unhappy feeling people have when they have done something wrong.

shampoo
1. a liquid soap for washing the hair.
2. to wash the hair.

shamrock   a plant like clover with tiny leaves, which grows mainly in Ireland.

shape   the form of a thing; its appearance.
The *shape* of the ball is round.

share
1. to divide into parts.
Share the sweets between you and Tom.
2. one of the parts into which a thing is divided.
Eat your *share* of the cake.

shark   a large, dangerous sea fish. It has very sharp teeth.

sharp
1. pointed; having an edge that can cut.
The cat's claws are *sharp*.
2. clever; quick in mind.
Jean has a *sharp* mind so she is quick to learn.

shave   to cut off hair with a razor.

shear   to cut the wool from a sheep.

shears   large scissors for cutting wool, grass or hedges.

sheath   a cover for the blade of a knife or sword.

shed   a hut usually made of wood, for keeping tools or storing things.

shapes

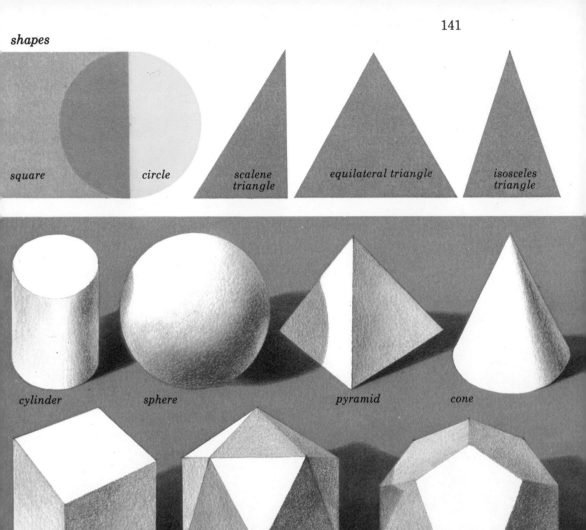

square   *circle*   *scalene triangle*   *equilateral triangle*   *isosceles triangle*

cylinder   *sphere*   *pyramid*   *cone*

cube   *icosahedron*   *pentagonal dodecahedron*

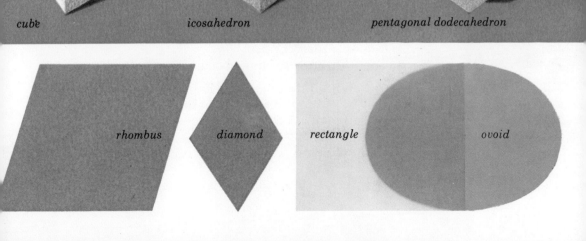

rhombus   *diamond*   *rectangle*   *ovoid*

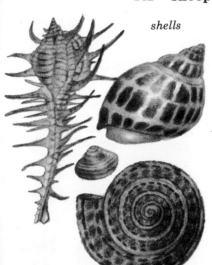

shells

sheep an animal whose coat gives wool and its flesh mutton.

sheet 1. a large piece of cloth used on a bed.
2. a thin, flat piece of material, such as paper or glass or metal.

shelf a board fixed to a wall for holding things.

shell 1. a hard outside covering as on an egg or nut.
Some sea animals and insects have a hard *shell*.
2. to remove the hard outside coverings as from peas or nuts.

shelter a place where people are safe from bad weather or danger.

shepherd someone who looks after sheep.

sheriff the person who keeps the peace in a county or district, usually in U.S.A.

shields

shield a shaped piece of armour carried to protect the body in battle.

shine 1. to give out bright light.
The stars *shine* in the night sky.
2. to polish.
Jane worked hard to *shine* the silver cup.

shingle 1. small stones on a beach; pebbles.
2. the covering for a roof.

ship a large boat that sails across the oceans.

shipwreck a ship that has been lost or destroyed; it may have sunk in a storm or crashed onto rocks.

shingle

shirt a piece of clothing made of thin cloth worn on the upper part of the body, usually by men and boys.

shiver to shake because one is cold or afraid.

shoal a number of fish of the same sort swimming together.

shock a nasty surprise.

shoe a covering worn on the foot.

shoot   1. to fire a gun or let loose an arrow.
2. to kick a ball at goal.
The striker was able to *shoot* at goal.
3. a small, young branch of a plant or tree.

shop   a place where things can be bought.

shopkeeper   a person who looks after a shop.

shore   land at the edge of a lake or the sea.

short   1. not very long or very tall.
This rope is too long. I need a *short* piece.
2. not lasting long.
This is a *short* poem.
3. not enough.
Mother was *short* of flour for baking.

shorts   very short trousers.
Footballers wear *shorts*.

shotgun   a kind of rifle that fires tiny balls of lead.

shoulder   the place where the arm is joined to the body.

shout   to speak or call out loudly.

shove   to push.

shovel   a tool like a spade but wider and with slightly curved sides. It is used for moving earth, sand and stones.

show   1. to let someone see something.
I'll *show* you my stamp collection.
2. to explain; to point out.
Mother will *show* me how to fry an egg.
3. an entertainment such as a play, or display such as a flower show.
We all went to a film *show*.

shower   rain, falling for only a short time.

shriek   a loud, high cry made by someone who is hurt or afraid.

shrimp   a small, grey shellfish which turns pink when cooked.

shrink   to get smaller.

shrub   a plant like a small, bushy tree.

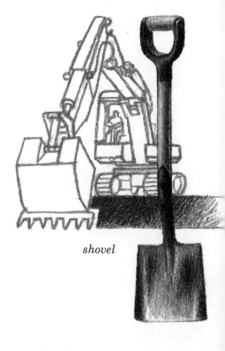

shovel

shrub

signs

Ancient Egyptian

zodiac

street

shut 1. closed, not open.
2. to close.

shy easily frightened away; not wanting to be with others.

sick ill, unwell.

side 1. the players in one team.
2. an edge; boundary.
He sat on the *side* of the pond.

sideboard a large piece of dining room furniture with cupboards and drawers for holding everything needed for the table.

sigh to breathe out heavily when one is tired, bored or sad.

sight 1. something seen.
2. the power to see.

sign 1. to write one's name.
2. a movement, such as nodding the head for 'yes', to let someone know something.
3. a notice that tells something, such as a traffic sign.

airport

Olympics

signal   1. a message given by signs.
The train stopped when the *signal* was at red.
2. to send a message by signs.

signpost   a post with a sign fastened to it, often used to give directions and distances.

silence   the lack of sound or noise; quietness.

silk   1. the fine, soft thread spun by silkworms.
2. the smooth cloth made from silk threads.

silly   foolish, not clever.

silver   1. a shiny, grey-white, precious metal.
2. things made from silver.

similar   alike; almost the same as something else.

simple   1. easy to do, not difficult.
2. silly, not clever.

sing   to use the voice to make music.

singer   a person who sings.

single   1. only one.
2. not married.

safety

ighway

country

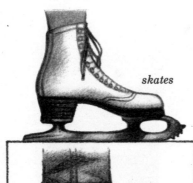

skates

ski

skin-diver

sink 1. to go down into the water or into the ground.
2. a bowl with taps and a drain.

sip to drink little by little.

siren a hooter or whistle making a loud noise.

sister a girl in a family where there is more than one child.

sit to be seated on a chair or some other seat.

size the space a thing takes up; the bigness or smallness of anything.

skate 1. a thin metal blade fastened to the sole of a boot for moving over ice (ice-skate); or rollers attached to a shoe for moving over ground (roller skate).
2. to move smoothly on ice or roller skates.
3. a flat sea fish.

skeleton all the bones in the body.

ski to move quickly over hard snow on two long pieces of wood called skis. They are fastened to special boots.

skid to slide suddenly on something slippery or very smooth.

skin the outside covering of a fruit or of the body of a person or animal.

skin-diver someone who dives and swims underwater often wearing flippers, mask and snorkel, and sometimes air cylinders strapped to the back.

skip 1. to jump lightly up and down on one leg at a time, often over a skipping rope.
2. to leave out something.

skipper the captain of a ship or boat.

skirt a garment or the part of a dress hanging from the waist, worn by women and girls.

skull the bones of the head.

sky the space above the earth where clouds, the sun, moon and stars can be seen.

skylark   a small bird which flies very high into the air and sings as it flies.

skyscraper   a very tall building.

slack   1. loose; not tight.
2. careless.
3. not busy.

slam   to close or bang something with a loud noise.

slap   to smack someone with the flat of the hand.

slate   a blue-grey rock that splits easily into thin pieces. It is used for roofs.

slay   to kill.
St George rode out to *slay* the dragon.

sledge   a low platform on runners that slides smoothly over the snow.

sledge-hammer   a very heavy hammer.

sleep   a time of rest when one is not awake.

sleet   rain mixed with snow.

sleeve   that part of clothing which covers the arms.

slice   a flat piece cut from something.
Will you have a *slice* of bread?

slide   1. to move very easily over a smooth surface.
2. a hair clip.

slight   small and slim.

slim   not fat; thin.

slip   1. to lose balance and fall.
2. a small mistake.
3. to go quietly and quickly.

slippers   soft shoes worn in the house.

slope   ground that goes up or down from a level.

slow   1. not fast; taking a long time.
2. behind the time.
Your watch is five minutes *slow*.

skyscrapers

slide

sledge

snail

snake

snorkel

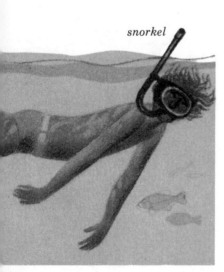

smack to slap someone with the open hand.

small not large; little.

smash 1. to break something into pieces.
2. to crash.

smell 1. what the nose tells one about something.
There is a *smell* of something burning.
2. to give out a smell.
These flowers *smell* sweetly.

smile a happy look.

smoke the dark cloud that rises from something burning.

smooth level; without any bumps.

smuggler someone who takes goods into or out of a country when it is against the law.

snack a small, quick meal, such as a sandwich.

snail a small creature that has a shell on its back and moves very slowly.

snake a crawling animal with a long body and no legs.

snap 1. to break suddenly with a sharp noise.
2. to try to bite something or somebody.
3. to speak in an angry way.
4. a card game played by children.
5. a photograph, short for snapshot.

snatch to grab something suddenly.

sneeze the sudden blowing noise made when something tickles the nose.

sniff to take in little, short breaths through the nose.

snooker a game played on a special table using coloured balls.

snore to make a loud breathing noise when asleep.

snorkel a tube used by swimmers to breathe under water. One end is above water, the other end is held in the mouth for breathing.

snow   soft, white flakes of frozen water that fall from the sky.

snowball   a ball made of snow pressed together.

snowdrop   a small, white flower appearing at the start of spring.

snowman   a figure of a man made of snow.

snowstorm   a storm when much snow falls.

soak   to make very wet.

soap   a solid or liquid used with water to make things clean.

soccer   football played with a round ball.

sock   a short covering for the foot and ankle.

sofa   a long, soft seat like a settee.

soft   1. not hard.
2. gentle and quiet.

soil   1. the ground in which plants grow.
Plant the seeds in *soil* in that pot.
2. to make dirty.
You will *soil* your trousers if you sit on the ground.

soldier   a person in an army.

sole   1. the bottom of the foot or shoe.
2. a flat sea fish.
3. only.

solid   hard and firm.
Water is liquid, rock is *solid*.

somebody   a person who is not named.

somersault   to turn head over heels in the air.

something   a thing not named or known.

sometimes   now and then; not all the time.

son   the boy child of a mother and father.

song   words and music together.

soon   in the very near future.

soot   the black dust which comes from burning coal or wood.

snowdrop

soccer

somersault

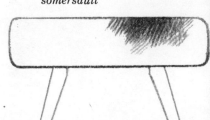

spaceships

sore   1. painful.
Bob's leg is *sore* where the ball hit it.
2. a place on the skin which is painful.
The *sore* on Anne's leg hurts.

sorry   1. feeling sad because one has done some-thing wrong.
2. feeling unhappy about something that has happened.

sort   1. to put things together that belong.
Sort these paints into their colours.
2. a kind or type.
What *sort* of sweets do you like?

sound   anything that can be heard.

soup   a liquid food made by boiling meat or vegetables or other foods in water or milk.

sour   not sweet to taste.
Lemons are *sour*.

south   one of the four main compass points; the opposite to north.

sou'wester   1. a waterproof hat that reaches down to the back of the neck.
2. a wind from the south-west.

sow (as in **now**)   a female pig.

sow (as in **go**)   to plant seeds in the ground.

space   1. the distance between things; a place with nothing in it.
2. the place far above the earth where there is no air.

space helmet   a covering for the head worn by space travellers.

spaceship   a special machine powered by rocket motors that travels into space.

spade   a tool used for digging.

span   the distance between the tips of the thumb and little finger when the hand is stretched out.

spark   a very small piece of something burning; a flash.

sparkle   to give off little flashes of light.

sparrow   a small brown and grey bird.

speak   to say something.

spear   a weapon with a long handle and a sharp metal point at one end.

special   made for a particular use; not ordinary.

speck   a tiny piece, often of dirt.

spectacles   glasses worn to help people to see better.

spectator   someone who watches others doing something,

speech   1. the sounds made when talking.
2. a talk given by someone on a special occasion.

speed   the rate at which something moves. The aircraft landed at low *speed*.

speedometer   an instrument to show how fast vehicles travel, such as cars, trains, lorries and motor cycles.

speedway   a race-track built for motor cycles and cars.

spell   1. to write or say the letters of a word in the right order.
2. words supposed to have magic power. The fairy cast a *spell* on the wicked witch.

spend   to pay out money.

sphere   a ball shape.

spider   a small animal with eight legs. It spins a web to catch insects for food.

spike   a sharp point.

spin   1. to turn round and round.
2. to make thread out of cotton or wool.
3. to make a web like a spider.

spine   1. the backbone of a person or animal.
2. a sharp spike on the back of an animal like a hedgehog or sea creature.

speedway

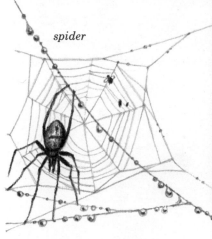
spider

spin

splashdown

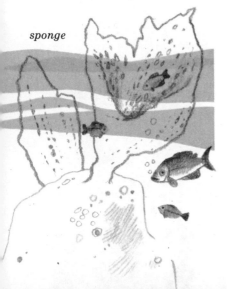

sponge

splash 1. to throw water about.
2. the noise made when someone or something falls into water.

splashdown the landing of a space capsule in the sea or ocean.

splendid excellent; beautiful; wonderful.

split 1. to break or cut something from end to end.
2. a long crack or tear or break.

spoil to damage something, so that it is sometimes of no further use.

spoke a thin bar or strong wire from the centre to the rim of a wheel.

sponge 1. a soft material with holes for soaking up water. It is used for washing.
2. a soft cake.

spoon a tool used for eating or stirring liquids or soft food.

sport games or pastimes, such as football, fishing, tennis and swimming.

spot 1. a small mark.
2. to see something.

spray 1. to send out tiny drops of water.
2. a bunch of flowers.

spread 1. to cover.
Mother began to *spread* the butter on the bread.
2. to stretch out.
The bird *spread* its wings and flew off.

spring 1. to jump or leap.
2. a piece of twisted wire that goes back into shape after it is pressed down.
3. the season after winter when plants start to grow.
4. a flow of water from the earth.

sprint 1. a fast, short race.
2. to run quickly for a short distance.

sprout 1. to start to grow.
2. a green vegetable that looks like a very small cabbage; a brussel sprout.

spur   a pointed instrument worn on the heel by a rider for making a horse go faster by pricking it.

spurt   a rush of liquid.
There was a *spurt* of water from the broken pipe.

spy   1. someone who secretly watches others to see what they are doing.
2. to see.

square   1. a shape that has four straight sides, all the same length.
2. an open place in a town.
3. to multiply a number by itself.
If you *square* 2, the answer is 4.

squash   1. a fruit drink.
2. to crush or squeeze.
3. a ball game.

squaw   an American Indian woman usually a wife.

squeak   a short, shrill sound.

squeal   a long, sharp cry.

squeeze   to press hard; to crush.

squirrel   a small grey or red animal with a bushy tail.

stable   a building where horses are kept.

stack   a large heap or pile.

stag   a male deer.

stage   a platform in a theatre or hall.

stage-coach   a large passenger coach pulled by horses. It used to travel across the country stopping at certain places to let people off or on and to change horses.

stain   1. a dirty mark.
The ink *stain* is still on your jacket.
2. to change the colour of something.
We can *stain* the wood to make it dark.

stairs   a number of steps in a building for walking up or down.

stale   not fresh.

squirrels

stagecoach

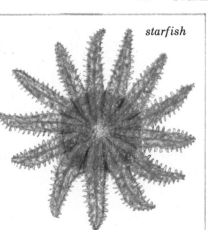

starfish

steamer

stalk   1. the stem of a plant or flower.
   2. to follow an animal to catch or watch it.

stallion   a male horse.

stamp   1. a small piece of paper to stick on a letter or parcel to show that a charge has been paid.
   2. to bang the foot on the ground.

stand   1. to be on one's feet.
   2. rows of raised seats, often under cover, from which people can watch sports.

star   1. a large object in space. It is seen as a bright point of light in the sky at night.
   2. a famous person such as a singer or actor.

stare   to look at anything for a long time with the eyes wide open.

starfish   a star-shaped sea animal.

starlight   light coming from the stars.

starling   a common wild bird with dark glossy feathers.

start   to begin.

starve   to be in much need of food and maybe die.

station   1. a place where trains or buses start from or stop.
   2. a building for policemen and firemen.

stationer   a shopkeeper who sells writing paper, envelopes, pens and pencils.

statue   a figure of a person or animal usually carved out of wood or stone.

stay   to be in one place and not leave.

steak   a thick slice of meat or fish.

steal   to take something which belongs to someone else.

steam   1. the white cloud seen coming from boiling water.
   2. to cook with steam.

steamer   a ship, driven by steam.

steel   a strong metal made from iron.

steep   sloping very sharply.
The boys climbed the *steep* hill.

steeple   a church tower with a high, pointed top.

steer   to guide anything such as a car or ship.

stem   the thin part of a plant that holds up the leaves or flowers.

steeple

step   1. a forward, backward or sideways movement of the foot; a pace.
2. one stair in a staircase.
3. a raised slab of stone in front of a door.

stern   1. strict; firm.
Dad called in a *stern* voice, "Come away from the pond."
2. the back end of a ship.

stew   to cook food, such as meat and vegetables, by boiling slowly.

stick   1. a long, thin piece of wood.
2. anything shaped like a stick.
A *stick* of rock or gum.
3. to fasten together with glue or paste.

stickleback   a small fish with spines on its back. It lives in rivers and ponds.

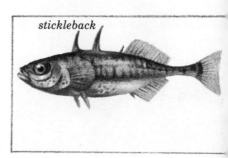

stickleback

stiff   hard; firm; not easy to bend or move.

stile   a step or steps used in going over a fence or wall.

still   1. not moving; quiet.
2. as before.
The street is *still* busy.

sting   a small amount of poison pricked into the skin by an animal or plant.
A nettle *sting* is painful.

stile

stitch   to join or decorate by using needle and thread.

stocking   a long covering for the foot and leg.

stomach   the part of the body that holds food after it is eaten.

stool

storm

strawberry

stone 1. a small piece of rock; a pebble.
2. the hard seed in the middle of some kinds of fruit such as the plum and peach.

stool a small seat with no back or arms.

stop 1. to finish what one is doing.
2. to bring to a halt; to come to a halt. John will always *stop* at the kerb before he crosses the road.

store 1. to put a thing away until it is needed.
2. a large shop.

stork a large bird with a long beak, legs and neck.

storm very bad weather with heavy rain or snow, strong winds and maybe thunder and lightning.

story a tale that can be either true or made-up.

stove 1. a cooker or oven for heating food.
2. a type of closed fire for warming a room.

straight without a bend or curve.
A ruler helps you to draw a *straight* line.

stranger someone not known.

straw dry stems of wheat, oats or other grain.
Farm animals sleep on *straw*.

strawberry a small, soft, juicy, red fruit with many seeds on the outside.

stream a small river.

street a road with houses, shops or other buildings on both sides.

strength being strong; a powerful force.
The elephant showed great *strength* when it lifted the tree trunks.

stretch to make something longer or wider by pulling.

stride to walk with long steps.

strike 1. to hit.
2. to light a match by rubbing it against a rough surface.
3. to stop work to put something right or to force a change.

string   strong, thick thread used for tying things.

stroke   1. to rub gently.
Watch the baby *stroke* the cat.
2. a blow.
Dad chopped the piece of wood in two with one *stroke* of the axe.

stroll   to walk along slowly.

strong   able to carry or lift heavy things; powerful.

study   1. to learn.
2. a room for quiet work.

stuffy   short of fresh air.

stumble   to trip over; to fall.

stupid   silly; foolish.

sty   1. a place where pigs are kept.
2. a small swelling on the eye-lid.

submarine   a ship which can sail underwater.

subtract   to take away.
If you *subtract* 6 from 8 the answer is 2.

subway   1. a kind of tunnel built under a busy road to allow people to reach the other side safely.
2. an underground railway.

succeed   to do what one sets out to do.

suck   to draw something into the mouth.

sudden   happening quickly; not expected.
The branch broke with a *sudden* crack.

suffer   to feel pain.

sugar   a food added to other foods and drinks to make them sweet.

suit   a set of clothes such as jacket and trousers.

suitable   fitting; right.
Whiskers is a *suitable* name for a cat.

sultana   a kind of grape that has been partly dried and is used in cakes.

submarine

subway

sunflower

supermarket

sum   1. the number made by adding two or more numbers together.
The *sum* of 2 and 3 is 5.
2. a problem in arithmetic.

summer   the warmest season of the year.

sun   the brightest object in the sky. It is seen in the day-time and it gives light and heat.

sunburn   a burning and redness of the skin after being in the hot sun.

Sunday   the first day of the week.

sunflower   a tall, yellow flower with a brown centre full of seeds.

sunrise   the time when the sun comes up.

sunset   the time when the sun goes down.

sunshine   the light of the sun.

supermarket   a very large shop where all kinds of food and goods are on sale.

supersonic   above the speed of sound.

supper   the last meal of the day.

sure   knowing that one is right; certain.

surf   large waves breaking on the shore.

surf-board   a shaped board used for riding the waves.

surface   the outside or top of anything.

surgeon   a doctor who cuts out or repairs bad parts in the body.

surgery   1. the cutting out or repairing of bad parts of the body.
2. the room where a doctor sees patients.

surprise   something that is not expected.

surrender   to give up.

swallow   1. a dark-blue and white bird with pointed wings and a forked tail.
2. to let food and drink go down the throat.

swamp   land which is soft and wet.

swan   a large, white bird with a long neck that lives on rivers and lakes.

swarm   a large number of insects or people. A *swarm* of bees settled on the tree.

sweat   the wetness that comes from the skin when hot.

sweater   a heavy, knitted jersey.

sweep   1. to clean using a brush or broom.
2. someone who cleans chimneys.

sweet   1. with a taste like sugar; not sour.
2. a toffee or piece of chocolate.
3. the pudding served at the end of a meal.

swell   to grow larger.

swerve   to move sideways quickly. The car had to *swerve* to miss the dog.

swift   1. quick.
2. a bird like a swallow.

swim   to move along in the water using the arms and legs.

swing   1. a seat hanging from ropes or chains.
2. to hang and move backwards and forwards.

switch   1. a lever for turning electricity on or off.
2. to change over.

swoop   to dive or move downwards.

sword   a weapon with a long, sharp, pointed blade.

syrup   a thick, sticky liquid made by boiling sugar with water.

table   a piece of furniture with legs and a flat top.

tablespoon   a large spoon used to serve food.

tadpole   a young frog or toad just hatched out of its egg.

tail   the part at the end of anything such as the tail of an animal, an aeroplane or a kite.

swan

sword

Tt

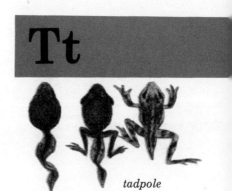
tadpole

tank

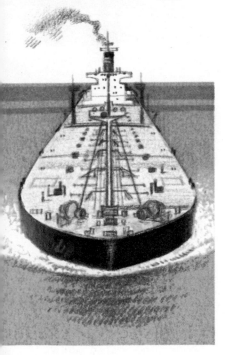

tankers

tailor   a person who makes clothes such as suits, trousers and coats.

take   1. to get hold of.
Please *take* this bag for me.
2. to carry away.
Did you *take* Tim's book yesterday?

take-off   the moment when an aircraft lifts off the ground.

tale   a story, usually not true.

talk   to speak; to use words.

tall   very high.
The giraffe is a *tall* animal.

talon   the claw of a bird of prey, such as an eagle or an owl.

tambourine   a small hand drum with jingling metal discs around the side.

tame   not wild; friendly.

tangerine   a kind of small sweet orange that peels easily.

tank   1. a container to hold liquids or gas.
2. an armoured car made of steel. It travels on tracks instead of wheels.

tanker   1. a ship that carries oil or other liquids.
2. a special kind of truck for carrying liquids.

tap   1. to hit something gently.
2. a handle that turns to switch on or off the flow of liquid or gas in pipes.

tape   1. a narrow strip of something such as cloth, sticky paper or plastic.
2. to copy a sound on a tape-recorder.

tape-recorder   a machine that copies and plays back sounds on a special kind of tape.

tar   a thick, black liquid made from coal or wood. *Tar* is used in making roads.

target   something to aim at.

tarmac   the tar surface on a road.

tart 1. a piece of pastry filled with jam or fruit.
2. sharp tasting; not sweet.

taste the sense in the mouth telling the difference between foods.
You can *taste* the salt in sea water.

tax money collected by the government to pay for things used by everyone, such as schools, roads and hospitals.

taxi a car that people pay to ride in.

tea 1. a drink made by pouring boiling water on the dried leaves of the tea plant.
2. a meal in the afternoon or early evening.

teach to show someone how to do something; to give lessons.
The instructor will *teach* you to swim.

teacher a person who helps others learn things.

teak a heavy, hard wood used for making furniture.

team a number of people or animals working or playing together.
The *team* of dogs pulled the sledge.
Derek is captain of the football *team*.

teapot a container with a spout and handle, used for making tea.

tear (as in **air**) to rip; to pull apart.

tear (as in **ear**) one of the drops of water that come from the eyes when someone cries.

tease to make fun of and annoy.

teenager someone between 13 and 19 years of age.

telegram a short message from one person to another sent by telegraph by the post office.

telegraph a way of sending messages quickly by electricity.

telephone an instrument that carries the voice through electric wires so that one can speak to someone far away.

tart

team

telephones

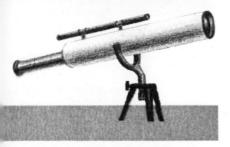

telescopes

tents

telescope an instrument with lenses which make things look larger and nearer.

television an electrical instrument that brings sound and pictures through the air from long distances.

tell to say; to give news of something that has happened.

temper the sort of mood one is in. You can be in a good *temper* or in a bad *temper*.

temperature the measure of how hot or cold something is.

temple a building where people worship and pray.

tender 1. soft; not hard.
2. loving. The mother looked after her baby with *tender* care.

tennis a game for two or four people, in which a soft ball is hit with rackets backwards and forwards over a net.

tent a shelter made of cloth or canvas held up by strong poles. Boy Scouts or Girl Guides often camp out in a *tent*.

term a period of time. We have examinations in the summer *term*.

terrible awful; dreadful. There was a *terrible* storm last night.

terrier a small dog.

terrify to frighten very much.

terror great fear.

test 1. an examination to see how much a person knows.
2. to find out whether something works properly. The plumber began to *test* the pipe to see if it leaked.

thank   to say one is pleased and grateful.
"*Thank* you for the present," said Peter.

thaw   the change from cold to warmer weather which melts snow or ice.

theatre   a building where people watch actors on a stage.

there   in that place; not here.

thermometer   an instrument to measure how hot or cold something is.

Thermos flask   a special flask that keeps what it holds cold or hot.
When Derek went fishing he took with him a *thermos flask* of hot coffee.

thermometer   *Thermos*

thick   1. wide or deep.
The castle walls were two metres *thick*.
2. closely packed; with few spaces.
A *thick* jersey keeps out the cold.
3. not flowing easily.
Syrup is a *thick* liquid.

thief   someone who steals.

thimble   a cover for the finger to help to press a needle through cloth.

thin   not wide or fat.
A sheet of paper is very *thin*.

think   to use the mind.

thirsty   wanting a drink.

thimble

thistle   a wild plant with a prickly stem and leaves. It is usually linked with Scotland.

thorn   a prickle or spike on a bush, tree or plant.

thread   a very thin, very long piece of cotton, wool, silk, nylon or any other fibre used used for sewing.

thrill   a feeling of excitement.
It was a *thrill* to watch the Olympic Games.

throat   the inside front part of the neck. It contains the tubes for swallowing air and food.

thistle

thrush

tiger

timber

through from one end or one side to the other.
Dad knocked the nail *through* the plank.

throw to send something from the hand into the air.

thrush a song-bird with a brown and white speckled chest.

thumb the short thick finger nearest to the wrist.

thunder the loud noise heard after a flash of lightning in a storm.

Thursday the fifth day of the week.

tick 1. the clicking sound made by a watch or clock.
2. a mark to show that work has been checked and is correct.

ticket a small piece of cardboard or paper to show someone has paid to ride on a bus or a train, or to watch a film or see a show.

tickle to touch or stroke lightly with the fingers so as to produce a tingling or itching feeling.

tide the regular rise and fall of the sea twice every day.

tidy neat, in good order.
How nice to see such a *tidy* desk!

tie 1. to fasten with string or ribbon.
2. a narrow piece of cloth worn knotted round the neck under a collar.

tiger a fierce wild animal like a very large cat. It lives in Asia and has striped fur.

tight fitting closely; not loose.
These shoes hurt me; they are too *tight*.

timber wood ready to be used in building or in making furniture.

time 1. the hour of the day shown on a clock.
2. seconds, minutes, hours, days, weeks, months and years.
3. to measure how long it takes someone to do something.

timid   easily frightened; shy.

tin   1. shiny white metal.
2. a metal can.
Mother bought a *tin* of sardines.

tingle   to have a prickly feeling.

tinker   a person who travels from place to place doing odd jobs for a living.

tinkle   to make sounds like a small bell.

tinsel   long, shiny strips of material used for decoration at Christmas.

tiny   very small.

tip   1. the thin end of something, usually pointed.
Hold the pen near the *tip*.
2. to overturn or upset something.
3. to give money to someone who has been helpful.

tiptoe   to walk on the toes.

tired   needing a rest.

toad   an animal like a frog, with a rough lumpy skin.

toadstool   a poisonous plant which looks like a mushroom.

toast   bread which is made brown and crisp by heating.

tobacco   a plant with leaves which are dried and cut up to be used for smoking in cigars, cigarettes or a pipe.

toboggan   a long, flat sledge, usually without runners, for sliding on snow.

today   this day; the present time.

toe   one of the five end parts of the foot.

toffee   a sticky sweet made from butter and sugar.

together   with someone or something.

toilet   1. a room where one washes.
2. a lavatory.

tinsel

toad

toadstool

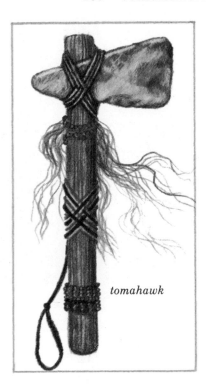

tomahawk

tomahawk   a kind of axe used by the Indians in North America.

tomato   a soft fruit with a red skin.

tomorrow   the day after today.

tongue   the thick moving part in the mouth used for talking and eating.

tonight   this night.

tonne   a measure of weight equal to 1000 kilograms.

too   1. also; as well.
Jack went to the circus. His brother went *too*
2. more than enough.
This rock is *too* heavy for me to lift.

tool   something which helps people to do work, such as a hammer, a saw, or a spade.

tooth   one of the white bones in the mouth used for biting and chewing.

toothache   a pain in a tooth.

toothbrush   a small brush with a long handle used for cleaning the teeth.

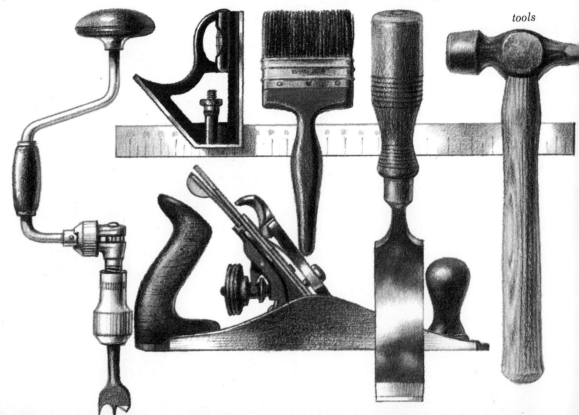

tools

toothpaste   a paste squeezed from a tube onto a toothbrush and used to clean teeth.

top   1. the highest part of something.
2. a spinning toy.

torch   a light carried in the hand, such as an electric torch.

torrent   a strong rush of water; a fast-flowing river or stream.

tortoise   a slow-moving animal with a hard, thick shell.

toss   to throw something into the air.

total   the full amount; everything added together.

touch   1. to feel something with the fingers or hand or some other part of the body.
2. to be so near that there is no space between.

tough   1. hard; not easily broken.
We could not eat the *tough* meat.
2. strong and brave.

tortoise

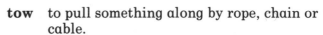

towers

tow   to pull something along by rope, chain or cable.

towards   in the direction of.
The rabbit ran *towards* its burrow.

towel   a piece of thick cloth used to dry wet things.

tower   a building, or part of a building, that is tall and narrow.

town   a large number of houses and other buildings together.

toy   something that children play with.

track   1. a narrow path through fields or woods.
2. railway lines.
3. a special road or path used for racing.
4. marks left by a person or animal.

tractor   a powerful vehicle used for pulling heavy loads and machinery.

trade   1. to buy and sell things.
2. the kind of work people do.
David's *trade* is painting and decorating.

traffic   everything that moves by road, by sea or by air.

traffic-lights   special lights that help to control traffic at cross-roads and junctions.

traffic-warden   a person who makes sure that cars are parked only in the permitted places.
A *traffic-warden* also helps to direct traffic.

trail   a track, such as footprints, left by a person or animal.

train   1. a number of carriages or wagons joined together and pulled by an engine on a railway line.
2. to teach; to practise.

traitor   a person who tells secrets to the enemy and betrays his country or friends.

tram   a kind of bus that runs on lines on a road. It is powered by electricity.

tractor

tramp　a person who wanders from place to place, begging and sleeping out of doors.

trampoline　a large piece of strong material fastened to a metal frame with springs. It is used for bouncing exercises and acrobatics.

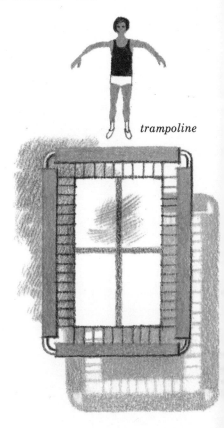
trampoline

transistor　1. a thing used to increase an electric current. It is used instead of valves.
2. a portable radio.

transparent　clear, easily seen through. A car windscreen is *transparent*.

transplant　to take out a plant from the ground and plant it in another place.

transport　to carry something from one place to another.

trap　1. to capture.
2. a hidden way of tricking people, or something for catching animals.

trapdoor　a door in the floor or ceiling.

trapeze　a swing high above the ground with only a thin bar for a seat.

travel　to go from one place to another; to make a journey.

trawler　a fishing boat that drags a large net along the sea bed.

tray　a flat piece of wood, metal or plastic for carrying food and dishes.

treacle　dark syrup made from sugar.

treasure　1. something worth a great deal of money, such as jewels or paintings.
2. to love very much.

tree　a very large plant with a trunk, branches and leaves.

tremble　to shiver or shake because of fear, excitement or cold.

trench　a narrow ditch dug in the ground.

trawler

tricycle

trout

trumpet

triangle   1. the shape made by joining three straight sides.
2. a musical instrument made of a steel rod shaped in a triangle and played by striking.

trick   1. a clever or funny act. The magician's first *trick* was to pull a rabbit out of a hat.
2. to cheat other people.

tricycle   a three-wheeled cycle.

trigger   part of a gun pulled back to fire the bullet.

trip   1. a short journey; an outing.
2. to catch the foot and stumble.

trolley   1. a small hand-cart.
2. a table or trays on wheels.

trolley-bus   a bus driven by electricity carried by overhead wires.

tropics   the very hot parts of the earth on either side of the equator.

trot   to run slowly.

trouble   anything that causes worry or unhappiness; difficulty.

trousers   clothing worn to cover the legs, usually from the waist to the ankles.

trout   a freshwater fish which is very good to eat.

trowel   1. a hand tool, shaped like a small spade, used for planting and weeding.
2. a tool with a flat blade used to spread cement and plaster.

truck   1. an open railway wagon.
2. a motor vehicle for carrying heavy loads; a lorry.

true   1. correct; real. It is *true* to say that $2 + 3 = 5$.
2. honest; faithful. The guide dog is a *true* friend to the blind.

trumpet   a musical instrument sounded by blowing.

trunk   1. the thick stem of a tree.
    2. an elephant's nose.
    3. a large box used for carrying clothes.

try   1. to do one's best; to attempt.
    2. to test.
    3. a score in rugby.

T-shirt   a light short-sleeved shirt or vest shaped like a T.

tube   1. a long, thin, hollow piece of metal, wood, glass, rubber or plastic.
    2. a container from which the contents can be squeezed, such as a tube of toothpaste.
    3. the underground railway in London.

tulips

Tuesday   the third day of the week.

tug   1. to pull hard; to pull with a jerk.
    2. a small, powerful boat which tows larger ships.

tulip   a spring flower that grows from a bulb.

tumble   to fall suddenly.

tumbler   1. a drinking glass.
    2. a person who can do somersaults; an acrobat.

turban

tuna   a large sea fish which can be eaten.

tune   a number of musical notes played one after another to make a pleasant sound.

tunnel   a passage cut through a hill or under the ground.
    Trains and cars go through a *tunnel* to get under a river or through a mountain.

turban   a long piece of cloth wound round the head and worn as a hat.

turkey

turkey   a large bird which can be eaten.

turn   1. to move round as a wheel does.
    2. to move left or right, or all the way round.
    3. a chance.
    It will soon be your *turn* to ride the pony.

turnip   a vegetable with a round, white or yellow root, which can be cooked and eaten.

turtle

tusks

typewriter

ukelele

turret   a small tower on a building.

turtle   an animal with a shell, like a tortoise. It lives in water.

tusk   a long, pointed tooth that sticks out of the mouths of some animals.

twice   two times.

twig   a very small branch of a tree or bush.

twilight   the dim light between sunset and darkness.

twin   one of two children or animals born at the same time to the same mother.

twinkle   to shine and sparkle in flashes like a star in the sky.

twist   to turn round and round.

type   1. a kind; a sort.
2. to print words on paper by using a typewriter.

typewriter   a machine which prints words on paper when keys with letters on them are pressed.

typhoon   a storm with very strong winds.

tyre   a strong rubber ring, usually filled with air, fitted round a wheel.

Uu

ugly   not pretty to look at.

ukelele   a musical instrument like a guitar.

umbrella   a shelter from the rain made of waterproof cloth stretched over a light metal frame and attached to a stick. It can be closed when it is not needed.

unable   not able to do something.

uncle   the brother of a mother or father.

under   below; beneath.

undercarriage   the landing gear, such as wheels, used by aircraft when taking off and landing.

understand   to know what something means.

undo   to unfasten, to untie or to open something.

undress   to take one's clothes off.

unequal   not the same in amount, size or number.

unhappy   sad; miserable.

unicorn   an imaginary animal like a horse with a horn in the middle of its forehead.

uniform   1. special clothes worn by people who belong to the same group, such as soldiers, sailors, airmen, policemen or schoolchildren.
2. exactly the same.

union   1. the joining together of two or more things to make one thing.
2. a group of workers who have joined together.

universe   everything that there is on earth and in space.

university   a place where people carry on their education when they have left school.

unkind   cruel; not kind.

unless   if not.
You will not be a good swimmer *unless* you practise hard.

unload   to take a load off something.
The men began to *unload* timber from the truck.

unlucky   having bad luck; out of luck.
Joan was *unlucky* today. She lost her new watch.

unnecessary   not needed.

unpleasant   not pleasant; nasty.

untidy   not tidy; not neat.

until   up to the time when; till.
Wait *until* you have eaten your dinner before you eat your sweets.

unicorn

uniform

upside-down

unusual   not usual; not very common; rare.

unwell   not feeling well; ill; sick.

unwrap   to take the cover off something.

uphill   up the slope of a hill; upward.

upon   on top of something.

uproar   a great noise of shouting and yelling.

upside-down   turned over the wrong way.
The cups are *upside-down* on the shelf.

upstairs   up the stairs; on the floor above.

urgent   very important and needing to be dealt with at once.

useful   helpful; of use.
A watch is a *useful* gift.

useless   of no use; worthless.

usher   a person who shows people to their seats in a cinema, theatre or church.

usual   almost always done; common; ordinary.

V v

valentine

vacant   empty; with nothing inside; not lived in.
The house next door is *vacant*.

vacation   a holiday.

vacuum   1. emptiness.
2. an electric floor cleaner which sucks up dirt.

vagabond   a beggar; someone who wanders from place to place.

vain   1. having a very good opinion of oneself.
Isn't Sandra *vain*? She is always looking in the mirror.
2. useless.
We begged Tim not to climb the mountain, but our words were in *vain*.

valentine   a card or affectionate greeting sent to someone on Saint *Valentine's* Day, 14th February.

valley   low ground between two mountains or hills.

valuable   worth much money; very important. A diamond ring is *valuable*.

van   a covered truck or wagon used for carrying things from place to place.

vanish   to go out of sight; to disappear.

various   of different sorts; several.

vase   a container for holding flowers.

veal   the meat from a calf.

vegetable   any plant other than a fruit that is used for food.

vehicle   a car, lorry, bus, wagon or sledge or any other means used for carrying people and goods from place to place.

vein   one of the thin tubes that carry blood back to the heart from all parts of the body.

velvet   a smooth, thick, soft, silky cloth.

venison   the meat from a deer.

veranda   a platform with a roof, built onto the outside of a house where people can sit.

vermin   certain small animals and insects such as rats, mice and fleas. They can do damage and may carry disease.

vessel   1. a ship.
2. a container to hold liquids.

vest   a garment worn next to the skin of the upper body.

vet   a short name for a veterinary surgeon; a person who looks after sick animals.

vex   to annoy someone; to make someone angry.

viaduct   a long bridge built to carry a road or railway over a valley or some other low ground.

vicar   a Church of England priest.

vegetables

bean

tomato

onion

mushroom

cabbage

aubergine

garlic

artichoke

Viking

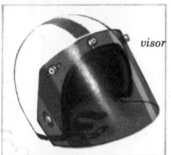

visor

volcano

victory   the winning of a battle or a game; a success.
Our last *victory* means that we have won the football shield.

videotape   a special kind of tape used for television, that shows pictures and gives out sounds when it is played through a special machine.

Vikings   warriors from north-west Europe who invaded Britain and other countries from the sea between AD 500 and 800.

village   a small number of houses and buildings grouped together, smaller than a town.

villain   a bad man; a wicked person.

vine   1. a plant that creeps along the ground or climbs up poles or a fence.
2. the plant on which grapes grow.

vinegar   a sour liquid used to add taste to some foods and for pickling.

violet   1. a small plant with purple, blue or white flowers.
2. a bluish-purple colour.

violin   a musical instrument with four strings, played with a bow.
The *violin* is held under the chin when being played.

visit   to call and see someone.

visor   the part of a helmet protecting the face. It can be raised or lowered.

vitamin   a substance necessary for health and growth, found in many foods.
Vitamin C is found in oranges.

voice   the sound made when speaking and singing.

volcano   a mountain which throws out hot ashes or liquid rock and steam through a hole at the top called a crater.

volume   1. a book.
2. the amount of space taken up by anything.

vowel   the letters *a, e, i, o, u* are vowels.

voyage   a long journey by sea.

vulture   a large bird that feeds on dead animals.

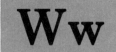

waddle   to walk like a duck, with short steps, and swinging from side to side.

wade   to walk through water that is not too deep.

wafer   a very thin biscuit.

wage   money paid for work done.

wagon   1. a cart used for carrying heavy loads. 2. a railway truck.

wail   to make a long, sad, crying noise.

waist   the middle part of the body between the chest and hips.

waistcoat   a short jacket without sleeves, usually worn under a coat.

wait   to stay in a place until something happens or someone comes.

waiter   a man who serves food to people in a restaurant or hotel.

waitress   a woman who serves food to people in a restaurant or hotel.

wake   to stop sleeping.

walk   to move about on foot.

walkie-talkie

walkie-talkie   a radio which can be carried about and used to send and receive messages.

wall   bricks, concrete or stones making the sides of a house, or a fence round a field or garden.

wallaby   a small kind of kangaroo.

wallet   a small, folding, pocket case usually made of leather or plastic and used for carrying money and papers.

walrus   a sea animal like a large seal. It has two tusks.

walrus

warehouse

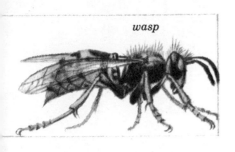
warship

wander   to walk about in no special direction. If you *wander* from the path you may get lost.

want   1. to wish for; to desire.
2. to lack; to have too little of something.

war   a fight between countries, or groups of people in the same country.

warder   someone who guards prisoners in a prison.

wardrobe   a tall cupboard where clothes are kept.

warehouse   a building where goods are stored.

warm   1. more hot than cold.
2. to heat.
Come by the fire and *warm* your hands.

warn   to tell someone about the possible danger of anything.
I must *warn* you never to play with fire.

warrior   a fighting man.

warship   a powerful ship that carries guns and other weapons.

wash   to make clean with water.

wash-basin   a bowl for washing the hands and face.

washer   1. a machine for washing clothes.
2. a round plate of metal or rubber with a hole in the middle used to seal or fasten.

wasp   a black and yellow flying insect that stings.

waste   1. to use something up or spend money carelessly.
Do not *waste* food. Do not take any more than you can eat.
2. rubbish; something that is of little use.
Please place your *waste* paper in the basket.

wasp

watch   1. a small clock usually worn on the wrist.
2. to look at something.
3. to guard.

weapons

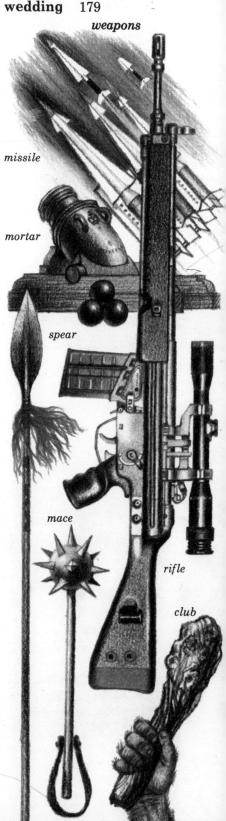

missile

mortar

spear

mace

rifle

club

water   1. the liquid in rivers, lakes, ponds and oceans; rain is water.
2. to wet with water.
Ruth is going to *water* the plants.

waterfall   a stream of water that pours from a high place.

waterproof   not allowing water to pass through.
Bill's raincoat is *waterproof*.

wave   1. a moving line of water on sea or lake.
2. to move up and down or from side to side.
Flags *wave* in the wind.

wax   a soft material coloured yellow that is used in making candles and polish.
Bees make a type of *wax* for their honeycombs.

way   1. a method of doing something.
A book tells you the *way* to build models.
2. a path or a road.
The *way* home is long.

weak   not strong.

wealth   a lot of money; many valuable things.

weapon   anything used for fighting or hunting.
A gun is a *weapon*, so is a sword.

wear   1. to have clothes on the body.
In winter you *wear* warm clothes.
2. to show signs of too much use.

weary   tired.

weasel   a quick-moving, small, thin animal that eats smaller animals such as birds and mice.

weather   how wet, dry, hot or cold the air is outside.

weave   to make threads into cloth.

web   a kind of net that spiders spin to catch insects.

wedding   the marriage of a man and a woman, when they become husband and wife.

oil-well

whale

Wednesday   the fourth day of the week.

weed   a wild plant that grows where it is not wanted in gardens and fields.

week   seven days.

weekend   Saturday and Sunday.

weep   to cry tears.

weigh   to find out how heavy something is.

welcome   to show pleasure when someone comes.

well   1. a deep hole in the ground dug to reach water or oil.
2. in good health.

wellingtons   tall rubber boots which keep the feet dry.

west   one of the four main compass points; the opposite to east.

wet   not dry; covered or soaked with water or other liquid.

whale   the largest animal. It lives in the sea.

wharf   a place where ships load and unload.

wheat   a plant whose seeds are used to make flour.

wheel   a circle of metal or wood which turns and helps things move more easily.

wheelbarrow   a handcart with two handles and one wheel.

while   1. during the time that.
While we were having our picnic it began to rain.
2. a space of time.
The accident held us up for a long *while*.

whimper   to cry softly.

whine   to give long, low, sad cries.
Dogs often *whine* when they are left alone.

whinny   the cry made by a horse.

whip 1. a piece of strong string or thin leather fastened to a handle and used for hitting.
2. to strike with a whip.
3. to beat eggs or cream very quickly.

whirlwind a very strong wind that blows round and round at great speed.

whiskers 1. stiff hairs growing on a man's face.
2. the long, stiff hairs that grow above the mouth of some animals, such as a cat.

whisky a very strong drink made from grain.

whisper to talk in a very quiet voice.

whistle 1. a sharp, high sound made by blowing through the mouth with the lips almost closed.
2. a small instrument for making whistling sounds when blown. The referee blew his *whistle* to stop the game.

whirlwind

white the colour of clean snow.

whole all; complete, with nothing missing.

wick the string which burns in candles and oil lamps.

wicked evil; very bad.

wicket the three stumps with two bails (small pieces of wood) on top, used in cricket.

wide stretching a long way from one side to the other; broad.

width the distance from side to side; breadth. The *width* of the river is fifty metres.

wife a married woman.

wig false hair to cover the head.

wigwam a hut or tent of poles covered with skins or bark in which some American Indians used to live.

wild not tame; fierce. Giraffes and lions are *wild* animals of Africa,

wigwam

willow

windmill

wilderness　a land where no people live; a wild place.

willing　glad and ready to do things.
Heather is *willing* to help her mother.

willow　a tree with narrow leaves and long branches that bend.
The wood of a *willow* tree is used to make cricket bats.

win　to come first in a game, a race or a competition.
I think Julie will *win* the prize for the best writing.

wind (as in **tinned**)　air that moves quickly.
The strong *wind* blows the leaves off the trees.

wind (as in **mind**)　1. to turn and twist; to move this way and that.
2. to tighten by coiling.
Remember to *wind* up the alarm clock.

windmill　a machine that is worked by the wind. It is used for grinding corn or for pumping water.

window　an opening, usually covered in glass, in the wall of a building to let in light and air.

wine　a strong drink made from the juice of grapes or other fruit.

wing　the part of a bird, insect, or aircraft that keeps them up when flying.

wink　to close and open one eye quickly.

winter　the season between autumn and spring; the coldest of the four seasons.

wipe　to clean or dry something by rubbing with a cloth.

wire　a long, thin piece of metal.
Wire carries electricity for electric cookers and refrigerators.

wireless   another name for radio; sounds sent from one place to another by radio waves through the air.

wise   sensible.

wish   to want something very much.

witch   a woman who is supposed to make magic.

wizard   a man who is supposed to make magic.

wobble   to move shakily from side to side.

wolf   a dangerous wild animal that looks like a large dog.

woman   a lady; a female; a girl when grown up.

wonder   1. to be curious about.
   I *wonder* what is behind that wall.
   2. surprise at something strange or unexpected.
   Paul's eyes opened in *wonder* as he watched the conjuror's tricks.

wood   1. a place where many trees grow.
   2. the part of a tree under the bark.
   Wood is used in the building of houses and to make furniture, boxes and many other things.

wooden   made of wood.

woodpecker   a bird that pecks holes in the bark of trees to catch insects for food.

wool   the soft, thick hair of sheep and lambs. *Wool* is spun into thread and used in making clothes and carpets.

woollen   made of wool.
   A *woollen* sweater is warm.

work   something to do; a job.

world   the earth, everything on it and in the sky above it.

worm   a small animal, with no legs, like a tiny snake. It lives in the ground.

worry   to be uneasy; to feel troubled.
   My parents *worry* if I am late in coming home.

witch

wizard

woodpecker

wreck

wrap   to cover something completely.
Ann uses pretty paper to *wrap* presents.

wreck   1. to destroy or damage badly.
2. something that is destroyed or beyond repair.

wren   a very small, brown song bird.

wrestle   to struggle with and try to force a person to the ground.

wriggle   to move by twisting and turning.
Worms *wriggle* along the ground.

wring   to get the water out of wet clothes by squeezing and twisting.

wrist   the joint between the hand and the arm.

write   to draw letters, words and figures so that people can read them.

wrong   1. not right or good.
It is *wrong* to steal and to lie.
2. not true; not correct.
Many of your answers are *wrong*.

x-ray   a ray which can pass through and photograph many solid things. It gives doctors a picture of the inside of the body.

xylophone   a musical instrument made of bars of wood which are hit with hammers.

yacht (as in **hot**)   a racing or sailing boat usually with sails.

yak   a long-haired ox found in parts of Asia.

yap   to bark sharply.

yard   a closed-in piece of ground usually near or round a house.

yarn   1. thread in long lengths made from wool, cotton and flax.
2. a story.

yawn   to open the mouth wide and breathe out, usually when one is tired.

year   a period of time; 12 months, 52 weeks, 365 days, or the time that the earth takes to go round the sun.

yacht

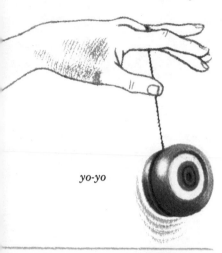

yo-yo

yell   to shout, scream or call out very loudly.

yellow   a colour.
Buttercup flowers are *yellow*.

yelp   a sharp cry or bark of an animal such as a dog.

yesterday   the day before today.

yet   up to now; so far.
The bus has not come *yet*.

yew   an evergreen tree.

yield   to give in; to surrender.
The soldiers would not *yield* to the enemy.

yoghurt   mildly sour thick milk, sometimes with fruit added. This word can also be spelled *yoghourt* or *yogurt*.

yolk   the yellow part of an egg.

young   not grown up; in the early part of life.

your   belonging to you.

youth   1. the time between childhood and being grown up.
2. a young man.

yo-yo   a toy shaped like a reel which moves up and down a string hooped onto a finger.

young

kitten

puppy

chicken

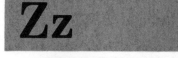

zeal   great enthusiasm.

zebra   an African animal like a horse with stripes.

zebra-crossing   a specially marked, usually striped, part of the road or street where people can cross safely.

zeppelin   a large flying balloon shaped like a cigar with engines and room for passengers.

zero   0; nought; nothing.

zigzag   moving sharply from side to side.

zinc   a soft, blue-white metal.

zip   a metal or nylon fastener with a sliding catch, used to fasten clothing and to close bags and purses.
Zip is a short word for zip-fastener.

zither   a musical instrument made of a flat box with many metal strings stretched over it. The strings are plucked to make musical sounds.

zebra

fawn

bear cub

piglet

zoo a place where wild animals are kept. People pay to go to see them.